Home-Based Bookkeeping Business Blueprint

Your Step-by-Step Guide to Financial Freedom and Success

Jeanelle K. Douglas

Copyright © 2024 by Jeanelle K. Douglas.

All rights reserved.

DEDICATION

To the reader who holds this book. You hold the key to unlocking this journey.

Thank you for joining me.

Table of Contents

Introduction to In-Home Bookkeeping Services 8

    Understanding the Concept of In-Home Bookkeeping 10

    Advantages and Challenges of Running a Bookkeeping Service from Home 12

    Market Demand and Potential Clientele 16

Assessing Your Skills and Qualifications 19

    Necessary Skills and Qualifications for a Bookkeeping Service 22

    Seeking Additional Training or Certifications If Needed. 25

Market Research and Target Audience Identification 28

    Conducting Market Research to Identify Potential Clients 30

    Understanding the Needs of Your Target Audience 33

    Identifying Niche Markets and Specialization Opportunities ... 36

Creating a Business Plan 39

    Importance of a Business Plan for Your In-Home Bookkeeping Service 42

    Components of a Comprehensive Business Plan 45

    Financial Projections, Budgeting, and Pricing Strategies 48

Legal and Regulatory Considerations 52

Registering Your Business and Obtaining Necessary Licenses 55

Understanding Tax Obligations and Regulations 59

Liability Protection and Insurance Considerations 62

Setting Up Your Home Office 68

Designing an Efficient and Professional Workspace 71

Selecting Essential Equipment and Software 74

Ensuring Data Security and Confidentiality 78

Developing Service Offerings and Pricing 82

Defining Your Bookkeeping Services and Packages 86

Determining Competitive Pricing Strategies 90

Offering Value-Added Services to Attract and Retain Clients . 94

Marketing and Promotion Strategies 98

Creating a Marketing Plan Tailored To Your Target Audience 102

Building an Online Presence through Website and Social Media 106

Networking and Collaborating With Other Professionals and Businesses 109

Client Acquisition and Relationship Management 112

Strategies for Finding and Acquiring Clients 115

- Building Strong Client Relationships and Trust 118
- Managing Client Expectations and Communication Effectively 121
- Bookkeeping Processes and Best Practices 124
- Establishing Efficient Bookkeeping Processes and Workflows 127
- Using accounting software effectively 130
- Ensuring Accuracy and Compliance with Accounting Standards 134

Managing Finances and Cash Flow 137
- Setting Up Financial Systems for Your Own Business 139
- Managing Cash Flow and Expenses Effectively 142
- Budgeting and Forecasting For Long-Term Sustainability 145

Scaling Your Business 148
- Strategies for Growth and Expansion 151
- Hiring Employees or Outsourcing Tasks When Necessary 154
- Leveraging Technology for Scalability 157

Managing Challenges and Risks 160
- Common Challenges Faced By In-Home Bookkeeping Services 163

Strategies for Overcoming Obstacles and Staying Resilient ... 166

Risk Management and Contingency Planning 170

Integrating Risk Management and Contingency Planning 173

Continuous Learning and Professional Development 174

Integrating Continuous Learning into Daily Routines 177

Importance of Staying Updated With Industry Trends and Regulations 178

How to Stay Updated 180

Participating In Professional Development Activities 182

Implementing Professional Development 185

Networking With Other Bookkeeping Professionals and Organizations 186

How to Network Effectively 189

Conclusion 190

Introduction to In-Home Bookkeeping Services

In the dynamic landscape of modern business, the need for meticulous financial management has become paramount. Small and medium-sized enterprises (SMEs), freelancers, and entrepreneurs alike find themselves grappling with the complexities of maintaining accurate financial records while striving for sustainable growth. Amidst this demand, the concept of in-home bookkeeping services has emerged as a beacon of convenience and efficiency. Imagine a scenario where professional financial expertise meets the comfort of home. In-home bookkeeping services epitomize this fusion, offering a unique solution to the burgeoning need for reliable financial management. At its core, in-home bookkeeping entails the provision of essential financial services from the cozy confines of one's residence.

The allure of in-home bookkeeping lies in its inherent advantages over traditional brick-and-mortar firms. By eschewing the need for a physical office space, entrepreneurs can significantly reduce overhead costs, thus opening the door to a more financially viable business model. Moreover, the flexibility afforded by operating from home allows entrepreneurs to strike a harmonious balance between work and personal life—a feat often elusive in the fast-paced world of business.

Yet, the appeal of in-home bookkeeping extends beyond mere cost-effectiveness and convenience. At its heart, this model thrives on the principles of personalized service and client-centricity. By working closely with clients in an intimate, one-on-one setting, in-home bookkeepers forge deep, meaningful relationships, gaining invaluable insights into their clients' unique needs and aspirations. This level of personalized attention not only fosters trust and loyalty but also sets the stage for enduring partnerships built on mutual respect and understanding. The journey towards establishing a successful in-home bookkeeping service is not without its challenges. Entrepreneurs must navigate a labyrinth of legal and regulatory requirements, ensuring compliance with tax laws and regulations while maintaining the utmost professionalism and credibility. Yet, for those willing to brave the waters, the rewards are boundless—a fulfilling career enriched by the satisfaction of helping clients achieve their financial goals, and the freedom to chart one's own path in the ever-evolving world of entrepreneurship.

In the pages that follow, we delve deeper into the intricacies of in-home bookkeeping, exploring the nuances of this burgeoning industry and providing invaluable insights into what it takes to succeed in this exciting realm. From market research and business planning to client acquisition and relationship management, this guide serves as your roadmap to realizing your dream of owning and operating a thriving in-home bookkeeping service. So, without further ado, let us embark on this journey together, as we unlock the secrets to success in the world of in-home bookkeeping.

Understanding the Concept of In-Home Bookkeeping

Understanding the concept of in-home bookkeeping entails delving into the essence of blending professional financial services with the comforts and efficiencies of a home-based setting. At its core, in-home bookkeeping represents a departure from traditional brick-and-mortar accounting firms, offering a more intimate and personalized approach to financial management.

An in-home bookkeeping service operates from the entrepreneur's residence, leveraging modern technology and communication tools to deliver high-quality financial services to clients. This model embraces the idea of flexibility, allowing bookkeepers to set their own schedules and work in a familiar and comfortable environment.

One of the primary distinguishing features of in-home bookkeeping is its emphasis on cost-effectiveness. Eliminating the need for a physical office space, entrepreneurs can significantly reduce overhead costs, including rent, utilities, and commuting expenses. This cost savings not only enhances the profitability of the business but also enables entrepreneurs to offer competitive pricing to clients, thus gaining a competitive edge in the market.

Moreover, in-home bookkeeping promotes a more personalized and client-centric approach to financial management. By working closely with clients in a one-on-one setting, bookkeepers can develop deeper relationships and gain a better understanding of their clients' unique needs and objectives. This intimate level of engagement fosters trust and loyalty, laying the foundation for long-term partnerships built on mutual respect and collaboration.

In-home bookkeeping also offers greater flexibility and work-life balance for entrepreneurs. By setting their own schedules and working from home, bookkeepers can better accommodate personal commitments and priorities, whether it be family obligations, hobbies, or other pursuits. This flexibility not only enhances job satisfaction but also contributes to overall well-being and happiness.

However, in-home bookkeeping embraces the principles of innovation and adaptability. In an increasingly digital world, entrepreneurs can leverage cutting-edge technology and software to streamline their operations, enhance efficiency, and deliver superior service to clients. From cloud-based accounting platforms to virtual communication tools, in-home bookkeepers have access to a myriad of resources to help them stay ahead of the curve and meet the evolving needs of their clients.

Advantages and Challenges of Running a Bookkeeping Service from Home

Running a bookkeeping service from home presents a unique set of advantages and challenges, each influencing the overall experience and success of the business.

Advantages:

1. Cost-Effectiveness: Operating from home eliminates the need for a dedicated office space, significantly reducing overhead costs such as rent, utilities, and commuting expenses. This cost savings allows home-based bookkeepers to offer competitive pricing to clients and increase profitability.

2. Flexibility: Home-based bookkeepers have the flexibility to set their own schedules and work hours, enabling them to better balance work and personal commitments. This flexibility is particularly beneficial for individuals with family responsibilities or other obligations.

3. Comfort and Convenience: Working from home provides a comfortable and familiar environment, which can enhance productivity and job satisfaction. Additionally, home-based bookkeepers have easy access to amenities such as kitchen facilities and rest areas, contributing to a more pleasant work experience.

4. Personalized Service: Home-based bookkeepers can offer a more personalized and tailored service to clients, as they have the opportunity to build closer relationships and better understand their clients' unique needs and goals. This personalized approach can lead to higher client satisfaction and loyalty.

5. Technology Integration: Advances in technology have made it easier than ever for home-based bookkeepers to leverage digital tools and software to streamline their operations and deliver efficient service to clients. Cloud-based accounting platforms, virtual communication tools, and online collaboration software enable home-based bookkeepers to work seamlessly with clients remotely.

Challenges:

1. Professionalism and Credibility: Operating from home may present challenges in establishing and maintaining a professional image and credibility, especially when compared to traditional brick-and-mortar firms. Home-based bookkeepers must invest in creating a professional workspace and presenting themselves in a manner that instills confidence and trust in clients.

2. Distractions: Working from home can sometimes lead to distractions, such as household chores, family interruptions, or noise from neighboring activities. Home-based bookkeepers must implement strategies to minimize distractions and maintain focus on their work responsibilities.

3. Isolation: Working from home may result in feelings of isolation or loneliness, as home-based bookkeepers may miss out on the social interaction and camaraderie found in a traditional office setting. It's important for home-based bookkeepers to find ways to stay connected with peers, colleagues, and industry networks to combat feelings of isolation.

4. Boundary Management: Separating work life from personal life can be challenging when working from home, as there may be a tendency to blur the lines between work hours and leisure time. Home-based bookkeepers must establish clear boundaries and routines to maintain a healthy work-life balance and prevent burnout.

5. Legal and Regulatory Considerations: Home-based businesses are subject to certain legal and regulatory requirements, such as zoning ordinances, business licenses, and tax obligations. Home-based bookkeepers must ensure compliance with relevant laws and regulations to avoid potential legal issues or penalties.

Running a bookkeeping service from home offers numerous advantages, it also presents its fair share of challenges. Proactively addressing these challenges and leveraging the benefits of a home-based business model, home-based bookkeepers can build successful and sustainable businesses that meet the needs of their clients while enjoying the flexibility and independence of working from home.

Market Demand and Potential Clientele

Market demand for bookkeeping services has seen a steady rise in recent years, driven by several factors including the increasing complexity of financial regulations, the proliferation of small businesses and startups, and the growing emphasis on accurate financial reporting for decision-making purposes. As a result, the potential clientele for bookkeeping services is vast and diverse, encompassing a wide range of businesses and individuals in need of professional financial management assistance.

1. Small and Medium-Sized Enterprises (SMEs): SMEs form the backbone of many economies worldwide, and they often lack the resources or expertise to handle their bookkeeping and accounting needs in-house. These businesses rely on external bookkeeping services to maintain accurate financial records, comply with tax regulations, and make informed financial decisions.

2. Startups and Entrepreneurial Ventures: Startups and entrepreneurial ventures are often focused on growth and innovation, leaving little time or expertise for managing financial matters. Outsourcing bookkeeping services allows these businesses to focus on their core operations while ensuring their financial affairs are in order and compliant with regulatory requirements.

3. Freelancers and Independent Contractors: Freelancers and independent contractors often have irregular income streams and complex tax situations, making professional bookkeeping services invaluable for managing their finances efficiently. From tracking expenses and invoicing clients to preparing tax returns, bookkeepers play a crucial role in helping freelancers maintain financial stability.

4. Professionals and Service Providers: Professionals such as doctors, lawyers, consultants, and service providers in various industries rely on accurate financial records to track income, expenses, and profitability. Bookkeeping services help these professionals manage their finances effectively, optimize tax deductions, and plan for long-term financial goals.

5. Retailers and E-Commerce Businesses: Retailers and e-commerce businesses face unique challenges related to inventory management, sales tracking, and transaction reconciliation. Bookkeeping services tailored to the retail sector can help these businesses maintain accurate records, monitor cash flow, and make informed inventory purchasing decisions.

6. Nonprofit Organizations: Nonprofit organizations have complex financial reporting requirements and must adhere to strict regulations to maintain their tax-exempt status. Professional bookkeeping services specialized in nonprofit accounting can help these organizations manage donations, grants, and expenses while ensuring compliance with regulatory standards.

7. Real Estate Agents and Property Managers: Real estate agents and property managers deal with numerous financial transactions related to property sales, rentals, and maintenance. Bookkeeping services can help these professionals track rental income, manage expenses, and maintain detailed records for tax purposes and financial reporting.

8. Health and Wellness Practitioners: Health and wellness practitioners such as chiropractors, massage therapists, and fitness instructors often operate small businesses and may require assistance with bookkeeping and financial management. Professional bookkeeping services can help these practitioners track client payments, manage expenses, and analyze financial performance to support business growth.

The market demand for bookkeeping services is driven by the diverse needs of businesses and individuals across various industries. As businesses continue to focus on financial transparency, compliance, and strategic decision-making, the demand for professional bookkeeping services is expected to remain strong, creating ample opportunities for bookkeepers to serve a wide range of clients and industries.

Assessing Your Skills and Qualifications

Assessing your skills and qualifications is a crucial step in determining your readiness to start and operate a successful in-home bookkeeping service. It involves a comprehensive evaluation of your expertise, knowledge, and capabilities in key areas relevant to the bookkeeping profession.

First and foremost, assess your proficiency in basic accounting principles and practices. A strong foundation in accounting fundamentals, including knowledge of double-entry bookkeeping, financial statements, and accounting software, is essential for success in the bookkeeping field. Evaluate your understanding of concepts such as debits and credits, accrual accounting, and financial reporting standards to ensure you have the necessary skills to perform bookkeeping tasks accurately and efficiently.

Next, consider your technical skills and proficiency with accounting software. In today's digital age, proficiency in accounting software is crucial for bookkeepers to effectively manage financial records, reconcile accounts, and generate reports. Assess your familiarity with popular accounting software programs such as QuickBooks, Xero, or FreshBooks, and determine whether you need to acquire additional training or certification to enhance your skills in this area. Evaluate your attention to detail and accuracy, as these qualities are paramount for bookkeepers responsible for maintaining precise financial records. Bookkeeping requires meticulous attention to detail to ensure that transactions are recorded accurately, accounts are reconciled correctly, and financial reports are error-free. Assess your ability to identify discrepancies, reconcile accounts, and troubleshoot accounting issues to determine whether you possess the level of precision required for the role.

In addition to technical skills, assess your communication and interpersonal skills, as effective communication is essential for building strong client relationships and providing exceptional service. Evaluate your ability to communicate clearly and professionally with clients, colleagues, and other stakeholders, both verbally and in writing. Consider your aptitude for listening, problem-solving, and explaining complex financial concepts in a clear and understandable manner to ensure you can effectively communicate with clients and address their needs.

Assess your organizational and time management skills, as bookkeeping requires the ability to manage multiple tasks, meet deadlines, and prioritize responsibilities effectively. Evaluate your ability to plan and organize your workload, maintain accurate records, and manage your time efficiently to ensure you can handle the demands of running a bookkeeping service and meeting client expectations.

Consider your commitment to ongoing learning and professional development. The field of accounting and bookkeeping is constantly evolving, with changes in regulations, technology, and best practices shaping the profession. Assess your willingness to stay updated with industry trends, participate in training programs, and pursue continuing education opportunities to expand your knowledge and skills and remain competitive in the field.

Necessary Skills and Qualifications for a Bookkeeping Service

To excel in the field of bookkeeping services, a comprehensive set of skills and qualifications is necessary. These skills extend beyond mere proficiency in numbers and financial software; they encompass a blend of technical expertise, communication abilities, attention to detail, and professionalism.

A solid foundation in accounting principles is essential. This includes understanding concepts such as double-entry bookkeeping, financial statements, and accounting equations. Bookkeepers must be adept at accurately recording financial transactions, categorizing expenses, and reconciling accounts to ensure the integrity of financial data. Proficiency in accounting software is also paramount. Bookkeepers should be familiar with popular accounting software platforms such as QuickBooks, Xero, or FreshBooks. Mastery of these tools enables efficient management of financial records, streamlined reconciliation processes, and generation of accurate financial reports.

Attention to detail is a hallmark of effective bookkeeping. Bookkeepers must possess a keen eye for spotting discrepancies, identifying errors, and ensuring the accuracy of financial records. Precision in data entry, account reconciliation, and financial reporting is critical to maintaining the trust and confidence of clients.

Communication skills are equally important in the realm of bookkeeping services. Bookkeepers must be able to communicate clearly and effectively with clients, colleagues, and other stakeholders. This includes conveying financial information in a concise and understandable manner, explaining complex concepts, and addressing client inquiries and concerns professionally. Furthermore, organizational skills are essential for managing the myriad tasks involved in bookkeeping services. Bookkeepers must be adept at managing multiple projects, prioritizing responsibilities, and meeting deadlines. Effective organization ensures that financial records are maintained accurately and that clients receive timely and reliable service.

Ethical behavior and professionalism are foundational to the bookkeeping profession. Bookkeepers must adhere to ethical standards and confidentiality requirements, maintaining the privacy and security of client information. Upholding professional integrity and honesty fosters trust and credibility with clients and contributes to the long-term success of the bookkeeping business.

A commitment to ongoing learning and professional development is crucial for staying abreast of industry trends, regulatory changes, and technological advancements. Bookkeepers should pursue opportunities for continuing education, attend training programs, and seek certification to enhance their skills and knowledge in the field.

The necessary skills and qualifications for a bookkeeping service encompass a diverse range of competencies, including accounting expertise, proficiency in software tools, attention to detail, communication abilities, organizational skills, ethical conduct, and a commitment to lifelong learning. By cultivating these skills and qualifications, bookkeepers can provide exceptional service to clients and build thriving businesses in the competitive landscape of bookkeeping services.

Seeking Additional Training or Certifications If Needed.

Seeking additional training or certifications is a proactive step for bookkeepers looking to enhance their skills, expand their knowledge, and stay competitive in the field. Depending on your assessment of your own expertise and areas of improvement, pursuing further education and certification can provide valuable benefits and opportunities for professional growth.

Here are some considerations for seeking additional training or certifications:

1. Identify Areas for Improvement: Based on your self-assessment, identify specific areas where you feel you could benefit from additional training or certification. This could include areas such as accounting principles, software proficiency, communication skills, or specialized knowledge in specific industries or sectors.

2. Research Training Programs: Research training programs, courses, workshops, or seminars that align with your areas of interest and development needs. Look for reputable institutions, professional organizations, or online platforms that offer relevant training and education in bookkeeping, accounting, and related topics.

3. Consider Certification Programs: Explore certification programs that are recognized in the bookkeeping and accounting profession. Certifications such as Certified Bookkeeper (CB), Certified Public Bookkeeper (CPB), or QuickBooks Certified ProAdvisor can enhance your credibility, demonstrate your expertise to clients, and open up new opportunities for career advancement.

4. Evaluate Costs and Time Commitments: Consider the costs and time commitments associated with pursuing additional training or certifications. Determine whether you have the financial resources and availability to dedicate to training programs, and weigh the potential benefits against the investment required.

5. Seek Recommendations and Reviews: Seek recommendations from peers, colleagues, or industry professionals who have completed training programs or obtained certifications in bookkeeping. Consider reading reviews and testimonials from past participants to gauge the quality and effectiveness of different training options.

6. Stay Updated with Industry Trends: Keep abreast of industry trends, advancements in technology, and changes in regulatory requirements that may impact the bookkeeping profession. Look for training programs or certifications that address emerging topics and skills relevant to the evolving landscape of bookkeeping and accounting.

7. Networking and Professional Development: Take advantage of networking opportunities and professional development events to connect with other bookkeepers, industry experts, and potential mentors. Attend conferences, webinars, or local meetups to expand your professional network and gain insights from experienced professionals in the field.

8. Set Goals and Track Progress: Establish clear goals for your training and certification efforts, and track your progress over time. Set realistic milestones and benchmarks to measure your achievements and ensure that you are making meaningful progress towards your professional development objectives.

Market Research and Target Audience Identification

Market research and target audience identification are critical components of launching and growing a successful bookkeeping service. Conducting thorough market research enables you to understand the needs, preferences, and behaviors of your target audience, allowing you to tailor your services and marketing efforts to effectively reach and engage potential clients.

To begin with, start by defining your target market. Consider the types of businesses or individuals that are most likely to benefit from your bookkeeping services. This may include small and medium-sized enterprises (SMEs), startups, freelancers, entrepreneurs, or professionals in specific industries such as retail, healthcare, or real estate. Once you have identified your target market, conduct market research to gain insights into their needs, challenges, and preferences. Utilize a variety of research methods, including surveys, interviews, focus groups, and online research, to gather information about your target audience's financial management practices, pain points, and priorities.

Explore the competitive landscape to understand the existing bookkeeping services available in your market. Identify your competitors, analyze their strengths and weaknesses, and assess the gaps or opportunities that exist in the market. This will help you position your bookkeeping service effectively and differentiate yourself from competitors.

In addition to understanding your target audience's needs and preferences, it is essential to assess market trends and industry developments that may impact the demand for bookkeeping services. Stay abreast of changes in regulations, advancements in technology, and shifts in consumer behavior that may influence the demand for financial management services.

Once you have gathered relevant data and insights through market research, use this information to refine your target audience and develop a marketing strategy that resonates with potential clients. Tailor your messaging, branding, and promotional activities to address the specific needs and pain points of your target audience, positioning your bookkeeping service as the ideal solution to their financial management challenges. Consider the most effective channels for reaching your target audience, whether it be through digital marketing tactics such as social media, email marketing, and search engine optimization, or traditional methods such as networking events, industry conferences, and local advertising.

Conducting Market Research to Identify Potential Clients

Conducting market research to identify potential clients is a systematic process that involves gathering and analyzing information about the target market to understand their needs, preferences, and behaviors.

Here's a detailed overview of how to conduct market research to identify potential clients for your bookkeeping service:

1. Define Your Target Market: Start by defining the characteristics of your ideal clients. Consider factors such as industry, company size, geographic location, and specific needs or pain points related to financial management. By narrowing down your target market, you can focus your research efforts more effectively.

2. Utilize Secondary Research: Begin your market research by gathering information from existing sources such as industry reports, market studies, government databases, and online resources. Look for data related to the size and growth of your target market, key trends and developments, and the competitive landscape within the industry.

3. Conduct Surveys and Interviews: Develop surveys or interview scripts to gather insights directly from potential clients. Reach out to businesses or individuals within your target market and ask them about their current bookkeeping practices, challenges they face, and what they look for in a bookkeeping service provider. Use open-ended questions to encourage detailed responses and uncover valuable insights.

4. Analyze Competitor Offerings: Research existing bookkeeping service providers in your target market to understand their offerings, pricing strategies, and areas of specialization. Analyze their strengths and weaknesses, as well as any gaps or opportunities that may exist in the market. This information can help you position your bookkeeping service effectively and differentiate yourself from competitors.

5. Explore Online Communities and Forums: Participate in online communities, forums, and social media groups frequented by your target audience. Monitor discussions related to financial management, accounting software, and bookkeeping services to gain insights into the challenges and pain points faced by potential clients. Engage with community members to build relationships and gather feedback on your services.

6. Attend Networking Events: Attend networking events, industry conferences, and business seminars where you are likely to meet potential clients. Take the opportunity to introduce yourself, learn about their businesses, and discuss their financial management needs. Networking events provide valuable opportunities to establish connections and identify potential clients who may benefit from your bookkeeping services.

7. Evaluate Online Search Trends: Use online tools such as Google Trends or keyword research tools to identify trends in online search behavior related to bookkeeping services. Look for keywords and phrases that potential clients may use when searching for financial management solutions. This can help you optimize your website content and online marketing efforts to attract organic traffic from search engines.

8. Assess Referral Sources: Identify potential referral sources within your network, such as accountants, business consultants, or industry associations. Reach out to these contacts and establish mutually beneficial relationships that can lead to client referrals. Referral sources can provide valuable insights into the needs and preferences of potential clients within their networks.

Understanding the Needs of Your Target Audience

Understanding the needs of your target audience is essential for tailoring your bookkeeping services to meet their specific requirements and providing value that resonates with them. Here's how to gain a deeper understanding of the needs of your target audience:

1. Conduct Market Research: Start by conducting thorough market research to gather insights into the needs, preferences, and challenges of your target audience. Utilize a combination of qualitative and quantitative research methods, including surveys, interviews, focus groups, and online research, to gather data directly from potential clients.

2. Identify Pain Points: During your market research, pay close attention to the pain points and challenges that your target audience faces in managing their financial records and bookkeeping tasks. Ask probing questions to uncover specific pain points related to accuracy, timeliness, compliance, or understanding financial reports.

3. Listen to Client Feedback: Actively listen to feedback from existing clients to understand their needs and areas for improvement. Solicit feedback through surveys, satisfaction surveys, or one-on-one discussions to gain insights into what clients value most in a bookkeeping service and where there may be opportunities to enhance your offerings.

4. Stay Updated with Industry Trends: Stay abreast of industry trends, regulatory changes, and advancements in technology that may impact the needs of your target audience. Keep an eye on emerging trends in financial management, accounting software, and industry-specific requirements to ensure that your services remain relevant and aligned with client needs.

5. Tailor Services to Client Segments: Segment your target audience based on factors such as industry, company size, and specific needs or pain points. Customize your bookkeeping services to address the unique requirements of each client segment, offering tailored solutions that meet their individual needs and preferences.

6. Provide Value-Added Services: Consider offering value-added services that address common pain points or add extra value for your clients. This could include services such as financial analysis, budgeting assistance, cash flow forecasting, or tax planning, depending on the needs of your target audience.

7. Communicate Clearly and Transparently: Clearly communicate the benefits of your bookkeeping services and how they address the needs of your target audience. Use language that resonates with your clients and highlights the value proposition of your services. Be transparent about your offerings, pricing, and processes to build trust and credibility with potential clients.

8. Seek Continuous Feedback: Continuously seek feedback from clients to ensure that your bookkeeping services are meeting their evolving needs and expectations. Use feedback mechanisms such as satisfaction surveys, client reviews, and regular check-ins to gather insights and make adjustments to your services as needed.

Gaining a deeper understanding of the needs of your target audience and tailoring your bookkeeping services accordingly, you can position yourself as a trusted partner who provides valuable solutions to your clients' financial management challenges. This customer-centric approach not only strengthens client relationships but also enhances the long-term success and sustainability of your bookkeeping business.

Identifying Niche Markets and Specialization Opportunities

Identifying niche markets and specialization opportunities is a strategic approach that can help differentiate your bookkeeping service and attract clients with specific needs or preferences. Here's how to identify niche markets and explore specialization opportunities:

1. Evaluate Industry Trends: Begin by researching industry trends and identifying sectors or industries that are experiencing growth or undergoing significant changes. Look for industries that have unique financial management requirements or face specific challenges that your bookkeeping service can address.

2. Assess Your Expertise: Consider your own expertise, experience, and interests when identifying potential niche markets. Reflect on industries or sectors where you have specialized knowledge or experience that could add value to clients. Assess your strengths, skills, and qualifications to determine areas where you can offer specialized services.

3. Consider Target Demographics: Explore niche markets based on demographic factors such as company size, geographic location, or client demographics. For example, you may target startups, small

businesses, solopreneurs, or specific demographic groups such as freelancers, creatives, or professionals in niche industries.

4. Research Untapped Markets: Look for underserved or untapped markets where there may be less competition and greater demand for specialized bookkeeping services. Consider emerging industries, niche sectors, or underserved client segments that could benefit from tailored financial management solutions.

5. Identify Unique Needs: Identify niche markets with unique needs or specialized requirements that your bookkeeping service can address. This could include industries with complex regulatory compliance, specialized accounting standards, or unique financial reporting requirements.

6. Explore Specialized Services: Consider offering specialized services that cater to the needs of specific niche markets. This could include services such as industry-specific accounting, tax planning, financial consulting, or software customization tailored to the unique requirements of clients in niche industries.

7. Analyze Competitor Offerings: Research competitors in your target niche markets to assess their offerings, strengths, and weaknesses. Identify gaps or opportunities where you can differentiate your bookkeeping service and offer unique value to clients in the niche market.

8. Seek Client Feedback: Gather feedback from existing clients or potential clients within niche markets to understand their needs, preferences, and pain points. Use client feedback to tailor your services and develop specialized offerings that address the specific needs of clients in the niche market.

9. Build Partnerships and Networks: Build relationships with industry associations, trade organizations, and networking groups within niche markets. Collaborate with industry partners, referral sources, or niche influencers to gain insights, access potential clients, and establish credibility within the niche market.

10. Stay Flexible and Adaptive: Remain flexible and adaptive as you explore niche markets and specialization opportunities. Be open to adjusting your approach based on market feedback, emerging trends, and changes in client needs to ensure that your bookkeeping service remains relevant and competitive in the niche market.

Identifying niche markets and exploring specialization opportunities, you can position your bookkeeping service as a specialized provider that offers unique value to clients with specific needs or preferences. This strategic approach not only helps differentiate your business in a competitive market but also allows you to focus your efforts on serving clients in niche markets where you can make the greatest impact and achieve long-term success.

Creating a Business Plan

Creating a business plan for your bookkeeping service is a critical step in establishing a roadmap for success and guiding your business operations. A well-crafted business plan serves as a comprehensive document that outlines your business goals, strategies, and operational plans, providing a framework for managing and growing your bookkeeping service effectively.

1. Executive Summary: Begin your business plan with an executive summary that provides an overview of your bookkeeping service and summarizes the key elements of your business plan. Include a brief description of your business concept, target market, competitive advantage, and financial projections to give readers a snapshot of your business.

2. Business Description: Provide a detailed description of your bookkeeping service, including the types of services you offer, your target market, and your unique value proposition. Explain the specific needs or pain points that your bookkeeping service addresses and how you differentiate yourself from competitors.

3. Market Analysis: Conduct a thorough analysis of the market for bookkeeping services, including industry trends, competitive landscape, target market demographics, and growth opportunities. Identify your target market segments, assess their needs and preferences, and evaluate the demand for bookkeeping services in your target market.

4. Competitive Analysis: Analyze your competitors in the bookkeeping industry, including their strengths, weaknesses, offerings, pricing strategies, and market positioning. Identify opportunities to differentiate your bookkeeping service and gain a competitive advantage, such as specialization in niche markets or offering value-added services.

5. Marketing and Sales Strategy: Outline your marketing and sales strategies for attracting and acquiring clients for your bookkeeping service. Describe how you will reach your target audience, promote your services, and generate leads. Include details about your pricing structure, sales tactics, and promotional activities, such as networking, referrals, digital marketing, and advertising.

6. Operational Plan: Detail the operational aspects of your bookkeeping service, including your business structure, legal considerations, staffing requirements, and workflow processes. Describe how you will deliver your bookkeeping services to clients,

manage client relationships, and ensure quality and accuracy in your work.

7. Financial Projections: Provide financial projections for your bookkeeping service, including revenue forecasts, expenses, cash flow projections, and profitability estimates. Use historical data, market research, and industry benchmarks to develop realistic financial projections that demonstrate the viability and growth potential of your business.

8. Risk Management Plan: Identify potential risks and challenges that may impact the success of your bookkeeping service and outline strategies for mitigating and managing these risks. Consider factors such as regulatory compliance, technology risks, staffing issues, and economic downturns, and develop contingency plans to address potential challenges.

9. Implementation Plan: Develop a timeline and action plan for implementing your business plan and launching your bookkeeping service. Define specific milestones, tasks, and responsibilities, and set deadlines for achieving key objectives. Monitor progress regularly and adjust your plan as needed to stay on track and achieve your business goals.

10. Conclusion: Conclude your business plan with a summary of the key points and objectives outlined in the document. Reinforce your vision for your bookkeeping service and emphasize your commitment to achieving success. Include any additional information or resources that may be relevant to investors, lenders, or stakeholders reviewing your business plan.

Importance of a Business Plan for Your In-Home Bookkeeping Service

The importance of a business plan for your in-home bookkeeping service cannot be overstated. A well-crafted business plan serves as a roadmap for your business, guiding your decision-making, setting clear objectives, and providing a framework for achieving success. Here's why a business plan is essential for your in-home bookkeeping service:

1. Strategic Direction: A business plan helps you establish a clear strategic direction for your in-home bookkeeping service. By defining your business goals, target market, competitive positioning, and growth strategies, you can align your efforts and focus your resources on activities that will drive success.

2. Goal Setting: A business plan enables you to set specific, measurable, achievable, relevant, and time-bound (SMART) goals for your in-home bookkeeping service. Whether your objectives include acquiring a certain number of clients, generating a targeted level of revenue, or expanding into new markets, a business plan provides a framework for tracking progress and evaluating success.

3. Risk Management: By conducting thorough market research and identifying potential risks and challenges, a business plan allows you to develop strategies for mitigating risks and overcoming obstacles. Whether it's regulatory compliance, economic downturns, or technology disruptions, having a plan in place helps you anticipate and address potential threats to your in-home bookkeeping service.

4. Resource Allocation: A business plan helps you allocate resources effectively and efficiently to support the growth and sustainability of your in-home bookkeeping service. Whether it's financial resources, human capital, or technology investments, a business plan ensures that resources are allocated in alignment with your business objectives and priorities.

5. Financial Management: A key component of a business plan is the financial projections, including revenue forecasts, expense estimates, and cash flow projections. These financial projections help you understand the financial viability of your in-home bookkeeping service, identify potential financing needs, and make informed decisions about pricing, budgeting, and resource allocation.

6. Communication Tool: A business plan serves as a communication tool for stakeholders, including investors, lenders, partners, and employees. By articulating your vision, objectives, strategies, and financial projections in a clear and concise manner, you can effectively communicate the value proposition of your in-home bookkeeping service and garner support from key stakeholders.

7. Continuous Improvement: A business plan is a dynamic document that can be updated and refined over time to reflect changes in the business environment, market conditions, and strategic priorities. By regularly reviewing and revising your business plan, you can adapt to new opportunities, address emerging challenges, and continuously improve the performance of your in-home bookkeeping service.

Components of a Comprehensive Business Plan

A comprehensive business plan is comprised of several key components, each of which plays a vital role in guiding the strategic direction, operations, and growth of your business.

Here's a detailed overview of the components of a comprehensive business plan:

1. Executive Summary: The executive summary provides an overview of your business plan, summarizing the key elements of your business concept, goals, strategies, and financial projections. It serves as a concise introduction to your business plan, highlighting the most important points and capturing the reader's interest.

2. Business Description: The business description section provides a detailed overview of your business, including its mission, vision, values, and legal structure. It outlines the products or services you offer, your target market, competitive positioning, and unique value proposition. This section sets the stage for the rest of the business plan by providing context and background information about your business.

3. Market Analysis: The market analysis section explores the market for your products or services, including industry trends, market size, growth opportunities, and competitive landscape. It identifies your target market segments, assesses their needs and preferences, and evaluates the demand for your offerings. Market research findings, industry data, and competitor analysis are used to inform the market analysis.

4. Marketing and Sales Strategy: The marketing and sales strategy outlines how you plan to attract and acquire customers for your products or services. It describes your target audience, positioning strategy, pricing strategy, distribution channels, and promotional tactics. This section also includes your sales forecasts, marketing budget, and plans for measuring the effectiveness of your marketing efforts.

5. Operational Plan: The operational plan details the day-to-day operations of your business, including your business processes, staffing requirements, facilities, equipment, and technology needs. It outlines how you will deliver your products or services to customers, manage your supply chain, and ensure quality and efficiency in your operations. This section provides a roadmap for executing your business strategy and achieving your objectives.

6. Financial Projections: The financial projections section presents your financial forecasts, including revenue projections, expense estimates, cash flow projections, and profitability analysis. It outlines your startup costs, funding requirements, and projected financial performance over a specific period, typically three to five years. Financial projections are based on assumptions and market research findings and provide a basis for assessing the financial viability of your business.

7. Risk Management Plan: The risk management plan identifies potential risks and challenges that may impact the success of your business and outlines strategies for mitigating and managing these risks. It assesses both internal and external factors that could affect your business, such as regulatory compliance, economic conditions, competitive threats, and operational risks. This section helps you anticipate and prepare for potential obstacles and develop contingency plans to address them.

8. Implementation Plan: The implementation plan provides a roadmap for executing your business plan and launching your business successfully. It outlines specific tasks, milestones, responsibilities, and timelines for achieving key objectives and milestones. The implementation plan helps you stay organized, focused, and accountable as you work towards your business goals.

Financial Projections, Budgeting, and Pricing Strategies

Financial projections, budgeting, and pricing strategies are essential components of any comprehensive business plan, especially for a bookkeeping service. They provide a roadmap for managing finances, allocating resources effectively, and ensuring the profitability and sustainability of your business.

1. Financial Projections: Financial projections involve forecasting your future financial performance based on assumptions and data collected during the market analysis and operational planning stages of your business plan. These projections typically include revenue forecasts, expense estimates, cash flow projections, and profitability analysis over a specific period, often three to five years.

Revenue Projections: Estimate your expected revenue based on factors such as the number of clients, pricing structure, average transaction value, and anticipated market demand. Consider different revenue streams, such as recurring monthly retainers, project-based fees, or additional services.

Expense Estimates: Identify your anticipated expenses, including both fixed costs (e.g., rent, utilities, insurance) and variable costs (e.g., software subscriptions, marketing expenses, professional fees). Be thorough in estimating expenses to ensure accuracy in your financial projections.

Cash Flow Projections: Project your expected cash inflows and outflows over time to ensure you have sufficient liquidity to cover operational expenses, investments, and debt obligations. Monitor your cash flow projections regularly and adjust as needed to maintain financial stability.

Profitability Analysis: Analyze your projected revenues and expenses to determine your expected profitability and return on investment (ROI). Identify areas where you can improve efficiency, reduce costs, or increase revenue to enhance profitability and achieve your financial goals.

2. Budgeting: Budgeting involves allocating financial resources to various business activities and initiatives in line with your strategic objectives and financial projections. A budget serves as a financial plan that guides your spending decisions, helps you prioritize investments, and ensures that resources are used effectively to achieve your business goals.

Start by creating a detailed budget that outlines your projected revenues, expenses, and cash flow for the upcoming period, such as a month, quarter, or year. Allocate funds to different categories based on their importance and urgency, such as marketing, technology investments, staff salaries, and overhead expenses.

Monitor your budget regularly and track your actual financial performance against your budgeted targets. Adjust your budget as needed to accommodate changes in market conditions, business priorities, or unexpected expenses. By maintaining a disciplined approach to budgeting, you can optimize resource allocation and maximize the efficiency of your operations.

3. Pricing Strategies: Pricing strategies involve determining the most effective pricing structure for your bookkeeping services to maximize profitability while remaining competitive in the market. Your pricing strategy should take into account factors such as the value of your services, the perceived quality of your offerings, and the pricing practices of competitors.

Consider different pricing models, such as hourly rates, flat fees, or subscription-based pricing, and choose the one that aligns with your business objectives and client preferences. Factor in your costs, desired profit margins, and market demand when setting your prices to ensure they are both competitive and profitable.

Differentiate your pricing based on the value you provide to clients, such as specialized expertise, exceptional service quality, or additional benefits offered. Communicate the value proposition of your services to justify your prices and differentiate yourself from competitors.

Monitor market trends, competitor pricing, and client feedback regularly to stay informed about changes in pricing dynamics and adjust your pricing strategy accordingly. Be flexible and responsive to market conditions to remain competitive and maximize your revenue potential.

Legal and Regulatory Considerations

Legal and regulatory considerations are essential aspects of starting and operating a bookkeeping service. Understanding and complying with relevant laws, regulations, and industry standards is crucial for ensuring the legality, integrity, and reputation of your business. **Here's a detailed overview of the legal and regulatory considerations you need to address:**

1. Business Structure: Choose an appropriate legal structure for your bookkeeping service, such as a sole proprietorship, partnership, limited liability company (LLC), or corporation. Each business structure has different legal and tax implications, so it's essential to select the one that best suits your needs and objectives. Consult with a legal advisor or accountant to determine the most suitable structure for your business.

2. Business Registration: Register your bookkeeping service with the appropriate government authorities to establish its legal existence and comply with regulatory requirements. Depending on your location and business structure, you may need to register with state or local agencies, obtain business licenses or permits, and fulfill other registration obligations. Research the registration requirements in your jurisdiction and ensure that you complete the necessary paperwork and procedures to legally operate your business.

3. Tax Obligations: Understand your tax obligations as a bookkeeping service provider and ensure compliance with federal, state, and local tax laws. Obtain an employer identification number (EIN) from the Internal Revenue Service (IRS) if necessary, and register for state and local taxes such as sales tax or business privilege tax. Keep accurate records of your income, expenses, and tax deductions, and file your tax returns on time to avoid penalties or legal issues.

4. Data Privacy and Security: Safeguard the confidentiality and security of client information by implementing appropriate data privacy and security measures. Understand and comply with data protection laws such as the General Data Protection Regulation (GDPR) if you serve clients in the European Union, as well as industry-specific regulations governing the handling of sensitive

financial data. Implement policies and procedures for data encryption, access control, data retention, and breach response to protect client confidentiality and comply with legal requirements.

5. Professional Liability Insurance: Consider obtaining professional liability insurance, also known as errors and omissions (E&O) insurance, to protect your bookkeeping service against potential legal claims or lawsuits arising from errors, omissions, or negligence in your work. Professional liability insurance provides financial protection and coverage for legal defense costs in the event of a claim by a client alleging financial loss or damages due to your professional services.

6. Ethical Standards: Adhere to ethical standards and professional codes of conduct in your bookkeeping practice to maintain integrity, trust, and credibility with clients and stakeholders. Follow principles such as honesty, integrity, confidentiality, and professionalism in your interactions with clients, colleagues, and regulatory authorities. Stay informed about ethical guidelines and best practices in the accounting profession, and uphold high ethical standards in your business operations.

7. Regulatory Compliance: Stay informed about regulatory requirements and compliance obligations relevant to your bookkeeping service, including accounting standards, tax regulations, and industry-specific regulations. Keep abreast of

changes in laws and regulations that may impact your business, and adjust your practices and procedures accordingly to ensure compliance. Seek guidance from legal and regulatory experts or professional associations to stay informed about regulatory developments and maintain compliance with applicable laws.

Registering Your Business and Obtaining Necessary Licenses

Registering your business and obtaining necessary licenses are critical steps in establishing the legal foundation for your bookkeeping service. By completing the registration process and obtaining the required licenses and permits, you ensure that your business operates legally and complies with regulatory requirements.

Here's a detailed overview of the process:

1. Business Structure: Before registering your business, determine the most suitable legal structure for your bookkeeping service. Common business structures include sole proprietorship, partnership, limited liability company (LLC), and corporation. Consider factors such as liability protection, tax implications, and

administrative requirements when choosing the appropriate structure for your business.

2. Business Name Registration: Choose a unique and memorable name for your bookkeeping service and verify its availability with the appropriate government authority. In most cases, you'll need to register your business name with the state or local government where you operate. Conduct a name search to ensure that your chosen name is not already in use by another business, and file the necessary paperwork to register your business name.

3. Business Registration: Register your bookkeeping service with the appropriate government authorities to establish its legal existence and comply with regulatory requirements. The registration process varies depending on your location and business structure. In general, you'll need to file registration documents with the state or local government, obtain an employer identification number (EIN) from the Internal Revenue Service (IRS), and fulfill other registration obligations.

4. Business Licenses and Permits: Determine the specific licenses and permits required to operate your bookkeeping service in compliance with local, state, and federal regulations. The licensing requirements vary depending on factors such as your location, business activities, and industry.

Common licenses and permits for bookkeeping services may include:

- Business License: A general business license may be required to operate your bookkeeping service in your local area. Check with your city or county government to determine the licensing requirements and apply for the necessary permits.

- Professional License: Depending on your jurisdiction, you may need a professional license or certification to provide bookkeeping services. Verify the licensing requirements with the appropriate regulatory agency or professional association and complete any necessary education or examination requirements.

- Home Occupation Permit: If you operate your bookkeeping service from your home, you may need a home occupation permit or zoning permit to comply with local zoning regulations. Check with your local planning or zoning department to determine the requirements and obtain the necessary permits.

- Tax Registration: Register for state and local taxes such as sales tax or business privilege tax if your bookkeeping service is subject to these taxes in your jurisdiction. Obtain tax registration certificates or permits from the relevant tax authorities and comply with ongoing tax reporting and payment obligations.

5. Federal and State Registrations: Depending on the nature of your bookkeeping service and your location, you may need to register with federal or state regulatory agencies or professional associations. For example, if you provide tax preparation services, you may need to register with the IRS and obtain a Preparer Tax Identification Number (PTIN). Research the federal and state registration requirements applicable to your business activities and ensure compliance with regulatory obligations.

6. Renewals and Compliance: Once you've registered your business and obtained the necessary licenses and permits, ensure ongoing compliance with regulatory requirements by renewing your registrations and licenses as required. Stay informed about changes in laws and regulations that may impact your business, and update your registrations and licenses accordingly to maintain compliance.

Understanding Tax Obligations and Regulations

Understanding tax obligations and regulations is essential for operating a bookkeeping service effectively and ensuring compliance with relevant laws. As a bookkeeping service provider, you are responsible for managing your own tax obligations and helping your clients navigate their tax requirements.

Here's a detailed overview of tax obligations and regulations that you need to understand:

1. Income Tax: As a business owner, you are responsible for reporting and paying income tax on the profits generated by your bookkeeping service. Income tax is calculated based on your business's taxable income, which is determined by subtracting allowable deductions from your gross revenue. Familiarize yourself with the tax deductions available to business owners, such as business expenses, depreciation, and retirement contributions, to minimize your taxable income and maximize your tax savings.

2. Self-Employment Tax: If you operate your bookkeeping service as a sole proprietorship or single-member LLC, you are subject to self-employment tax, which covers Social Security and Medicare taxes for self-employed individuals. Self-employment tax is

calculated based on your net earnings from self-employment and is reported on your personal income tax return. Be aware of your self-employment tax obligations and budget accordingly to ensure that you can cover your tax liabilities.

3. Estimated Taxes: As a self-employed individual, you may be required to make estimated tax payments throughout the year to cover your income and self-employment tax liabilities. Estimated tax payments are typically made quarterly and are based on your projected income for the year. Use Form 1040-ES to calculate and pay your estimated taxes, and stay current with your estimated tax payments to avoid penalties and interest for underpayment.

4. Sales Tax: Depending on your location and the nature of your bookkeeping services, you may be required to collect and remit sales tax on behalf of your clients. Sales tax regulations vary by state and locality, so it's important to understand the sales tax requirements in your jurisdiction and comply with applicable laws. Register for a sales tax permit with the appropriate tax authority, collect sales tax from clients when required, and remit the collected taxes to the tax authority on time.

5. Tax Reporting and Filing: Keep accurate records of your business income, expenses, and tax deductions throughout the year to facilitate tax reporting and filing. Use accounting software or bookkeeping tools to track your financial transactions and maintain

organized records for tax purposes. File your federal income tax return using Form 1040 or Form 1065 (for partnerships), and any required state or local tax returns, by the applicable deadlines to avoid late filing penalties.

6. Tax Deductions: Take advantage of tax deductions and credits available to small business owners to minimize your tax liability and maximize your tax savings. Common tax deductions for bookkeeping service providers include deductions for business expenses such as office supplies, software subscriptions, professional fees, and mileage. Keep detailed records of your business expenses and consult with a tax professional to identify eligible deductions and optimize your tax strategy.

7. Tax Planning: Engage in tax planning throughout the year to optimize your tax strategy and minimize your tax liability. Consider factors such as business income, deductions, credits, and tax law changes when planning your tax strategy. Consult with a tax advisor or accountant to develop a tax planning strategy tailored to your business needs and objectives.

8. Client Tax Obligations: As a bookkeeping service provider, you play a crucial role in helping your clients understand and comply with their tax obligations. Provide guidance and support to your clients on tax-related matters, such as recordkeeping, tax deductions, estimated tax payments, and tax filing requirements.

Stay informed about changes in tax laws and regulations that may impact your clients, and proactively communicate relevant updates and information to ensure compliance.

Understanding tax obligations and regulations, you can effectively manage your own tax affairs and provide valuable support to your clients in navigating their tax responsibilities. Stay informed about changes in tax laws and regulations, maintain accurate records, and seek guidance from tax professionals or regulatory experts as needed to ensure compliance and minimize tax risks for your bookkeeping service and your clients.

Liability Protection and Insurance Considerations

Liability protection and insurance considerations are critical aspects of managing risk and protecting your bookkeeping service from potential legal and financial liabilities. As a business owner, it's important to understand the various types of liability and risks associated with operating a bookkeeping service, as well as the insurance options available to mitigate those risks.

Here's a detailed overview of liability protection and insurance considerations for your bookkeeping service:

1. Types of Liability:

- Professional Liability: Professional liability, also known as errors and omissions (E&O) liability, arises from errors, omissions, or negligence in the performance of professional services. As a bookkeeping service provider, you may be held liable for financial losses or damages resulting from mistakes in your work, such as inaccuracies in financial records or incorrect tax filings.

- General Liability: General liability covers a broad range of potential risks, including bodily injury, property damage, and advertising injury. While bookkeeping services may not face significant physical risks, general liability insurance can provide coverage for third-party claims arising from accidents, injuries, or property damage that occur on your business premises or as a result of your business operations.

2. Professional Liability Insurance (E&O):

- Professional liability insurance, also known as errors and omissions (E&O) insurance, is designed to protect businesses and professionals from liability arising from errors, omissions, or negligence in the performance of professional services. Professional liability insurance provides coverage for legal defense costs, settlements, and judgments resulting from claims alleging financial loss or damages due to errors in your work.

- As a bookkeeping service provider, professional liability insurance is essential for protecting your business from potential claims or lawsuits arising from mistakes in your bookkeeping services, such as inaccuracies in financial statements, errors in tax filings, or failure to meet client expectations.

3. General Liability Insurance:

- General liability insurance provides coverage for a broad range of potential risks, including bodily injury, property damage, and advertising injury. While bookkeeping services may not face significant physical risks, general liability insurance can provide coverage for third-party claims arising from accidents, injuries, or property damage that occur on your business premises or as a result of your business operations.

- General liability insurance also typically includes coverage for legal defense costs, settlements, and judgments resulting from covered claims. By obtaining general liability insurance, you can protect your bookkeeping service from potential financial liabilities associated with third-party claims.

4. Business Owner's Policy (BOP):

- A business owner's policy (BOP) combines general liability insurance and property insurance into a single package, providing comprehensive coverage for common risks faced by small businesses. In addition to general liability coverage, a BOP may include coverage for property damage, business interruption, and other types of business risks.

- Consider purchasing a BOP to obtain comprehensive coverage for your bookkeeping service, including protection against liability claims and property damage. A BOP can provide peace of mind and financial protection for your business in the event of unexpected accidents, injuries, or property losses.

5. Cyber Liability Insurance:

- Cyber liability insurance provides coverage for expenses and damages resulting from data breaches, cyberattacks, or other cybersecurity incidents. As a bookkeeping service provider, you may handle sensitive financial information and client data, making you vulnerable to cyber threats such as data breaches or ransomware attacks.

- Consider obtaining cyber liability insurance to protect your bookkeeping service from potential financial losses and reputational damage associated with cybersecurity incidents. Cyber liability insurance can provide coverage for costs such as data breach response, forensic investigations, notification expenses, and legal defense costs.

6. Workers' Compensation Insurance:

- Workers' compensation insurance provides coverage for medical expenses, lost wages, and other benefits for employees who are injured or become ill as a result of their work. While bookkeeping services may not have significant physical risks, workers' compensation insurance may still be required if you have employees working for your business.

- Check the workers' compensation requirements in your jurisdiction to determine if you are required to carry workers' compensation insurance for your bookkeeping service. Even if not required by law, consider obtaining workers' compensation insurance to protect your employees and your business from potential liabilities associated with workplace injuries or illnesses.

7. Other Insurance Considerations:

- In addition to professional liability, general liability, cyber liability, and workers' compensation insurance, consider other types of insurance coverage that may be relevant to your bookkeeping service, such as commercial property insurance, business interruption insurance, or employment practices liability insurance.

- Review your insurance needs with an insurance agent or broker who specializes in business insurance to assess your risks and determine the appropriate coverage for your bookkeeping service. Consider factors such as the size of your business, the nature of your operations, and the specific risks you face when selecting insurance coverage.

Understanding the various types of liability and risks associated with operating a bookkeeping service and obtaining appropriate insurance coverage, you can protect your business from potential legal and financial liabilities and safeguard your assets and reputation. Prioritize liability protection and insurance considerations as part of your risk management strategy to ensure the long-term success and sustainability of your bookkeeping service.

Setting Up Your Home Office

Setting up a home office for your bookkeeping service is an important step in creating a productive and professional work environment. Whether you're starting a new business or transitioning to remote work, designing an effective home office space can enhance your efficiency, creativity, and overall well-being.

Here's a detailed overview of setting up your home office:

1. Selecting a Location: Choose a suitable location within your home for your home office. Consider factors such as noise levels, natural light, privacy, and accessibility when selecting a space. Ideally, your home office should be located in a quiet area away from distractions, with ample natural light and sufficient space to accommodate your work activities.

2. Designing the Layout: Plan the layout of your home office to optimize functionality and productivity. Arrange your furniture and equipment in a way that promotes efficient workflow and minimizes clutter. Consider ergonomic principles when selecting office

furniture and positioning your computer, desk, chair, and other work essentials to ensure comfort and support during long hours of work.

3. Creating a Comfortable Work Environment: Create a comfortable and inviting work environment in your home office to enhance productivity and well-being. Choose ergonomic furniture, such as an adjustable chair and ergonomic keyboard, to support good posture and reduce the risk of strain or injury. Personalize your workspace with decor, plants, and lighting to create a pleasant and inspiring atmosphere that fosters creativity and focus.

4. Organizing Your Workspace: Establish an organized system for managing your workspace and maintaining order in your home office. Invest in storage solutions such as shelves, cabinets, and file organizers to keep your desk and workspace clutter-free. Use labels, folders, and digital tools to organize documents, files, and supplies for easy access and retrieval.

5. Setting Up Technology: Equip your home office with the necessary technology and equipment to support your bookkeeping work. Install a reliable computer, high-speed internet connection, printer, scanner, and other essential tools and software for managing financial records, communicating with clients, and conducting business operations. Ensure that your technology is up-to-date, secure, and backed up regularly to protect your data and minimize downtime.

6. Establishing Communication Channels: Set up communication channels and tools to stay connected with clients, colleagues, and stakeholders. Use email, phone, video conferencing, and collaboration platforms to communicate effectively and efficiently with clients and team members. Establish clear communication protocols and response times to manage client inquiries, requests, and deadlines.

7. Creating a Distraction-Free Zone: Minimize distractions and interruptions in your home office to maintain focus and productivity. Set boundaries with family members and household members to respect your work time and space. Establish a daily routine and schedule to structure your workday and prioritize important tasks. Use productivity techniques such as time blocking, task batching, and the Pomodoro technique to manage your time effectively and stay focused on your work.

8. Promoting Work-Life Balance: Maintain a healthy work-life balance while working from home by establishing boundaries between your work and personal life. Set designated work hours and stick to a regular schedule to create structure and routine in your day. Take regular breaks to rest, recharge, and avoid burnout. Create boundaries between your home office and living spaces to separate work time from leisure time and maintain a sense of balance and well-being.

Designing an Efficient and Professional Workspace

Designing an efficient and professional workspace is essential for creating a productive and conducive environment for your bookkeeping service.

Here's a detailed overview of how to design an efficient and professional workspace:

1. Choose the Right Location: Select a quiet and dedicated area within your home for your workspace. Ideally, choose a location with natural light and minimal distractions. Consider factors such as proximity to amenities, privacy, and accessibility when choosing the location for your workspace.

2. Invest in Quality Furniture: Invest in ergonomic furniture that supports good posture and comfort during long hours of work. Choose a sturdy and adjustable desk and chair that can accommodate your work needs and provide adequate support. Consider additional furniture such as bookshelves, cabinets, and storage units to keep your workspace organized and clutter-free.

3. Organize Your Workspace: Keep your workspace organized and clutter-free to maximize efficiency and productivity. Use storage solutions such as shelves, drawers, and bins to store documents,

supplies, and equipment. Implement a filing system to organize paperwork and files for easy access and retrieval. Keep frequently used items within reach and designate specific areas for different tasks to streamline workflow.

4. Maximize Natural Light: Maximize natural light in your workspace to create a bright and inviting atmosphere. Position your desk near a window to take advantage of natural daylight and reduce the need for artificial lighting. Use window treatments such as blinds or curtains to control glare and maintain privacy while still allowing natural light to enter your workspace.

5. Upgrade Your Technology: Invest in reliable technology and equipment to support your bookkeeping work. Ensure that you have a fast and stable internet connection, a reliable computer, and necessary software applications for managing financial records and communicating with clients. Consider additional peripherals such as a printer, scanner, and headset for enhanced functionality and efficiency.

6. Create a Professional Atmosphere: Create a professional atmosphere in your workspace to convey credibility and competence to clients and colleagues. Choose neutral colors and tasteful decor to create a clean and professional aesthetic. Display diplomas, certifications, and awards to showcase your expertise and

qualifications. Keep personal items to a minimum to maintain a professional appearance.

7. Minimize Distractions: Minimize distractions in your workspace to maintain focus and concentration during work hours. Establish boundaries with family members and household members to respect your work time and space. Use noise-cancelling headphones or white noise machines to block out distractions and create a quiet work environment. Set specific work hours and adhere to a regular schedule to stay disciplined and focused on your tasks.

8. Stay Organized Digitally: Keep your digital workspace organized and clutter-free to improve efficiency and productivity. Use digital tools such as cloud storage, project management software, and task management apps to organize files, collaborate with clients, and track deadlines. Implement digital filing systems and naming conventions to maintain consistency and accessibility of digital documents and records.

9. Prioritize Comfort and Well-being: Prioritize comfort and well-being in your workspace to support long-term productivity and health. Invest in ergonomic accessories such as a keyboard tray, wrist rest, and monitor stand to reduce strain and discomfort. Take regular breaks to stretch, move around, and rest your eyes to prevent fatigue and promote physical well-being. Incorporate plants,

artwork, and personal touches to create a pleasant and inspiring work environment that enhances your mood and motivation.

Selecting Essential Equipment and Software

Selecting essential equipment and software is crucial for setting up your bookkeeping service and ensuring efficient and effective operations.

Here's a detailed overview of the essential equipment and software you'll need:

1. Computer: A reliable computer is the backbone of your bookkeeping service. Choose a desktop or laptop computer with sufficient processing power, memory, and storage capacity to handle your accounting software and other applications. Consider factors such as portability, battery life, and screen size when selecting a laptop for remote work or on-the-go tasks.

2. Accounting Software: Invest in accounting software to manage financial transactions, create invoices, track expenses, and generate financial reports for your clients. Popular accounting software options for small businesses and freelance bookkeepers include

QuickBooks, Xero, FreshBooks, and Wave. Choose a software platform that meets your business needs, budget, and level of expertise, and familiarize yourself with its features and functionalities to maximize efficiency and accuracy in your bookkeeping tasks.

3. Cloud Storage: Use cloud storage services to store and backup your accounting data, client files, and important documents securely in the cloud. Cloud storage solutions such as Google Drive, Dropbox, Microsoft OneDrive, or Box offer convenient access to your files from anywhere, anytime, and provide robust security features to protect your data from loss or theft. Choose a cloud storage provider that offers ample storage space, encryption, and data protection capabilities to safeguard your sensitive information.

4. Scanner and Printer: Invest in a reliable scanner and printer to digitize paper documents, receipts, and invoices and create hard copies of financial reports, client contracts, and other important documents. Look for a multifunction printer that combines printing, scanning, copying, and faxing capabilities for added versatility and efficiency. Choose a scanner with automatic document feeder (ADF) functionality and optical character recognition (OCR) technology for fast and accurate document scanning and digitization.

5. Internet Connection: A high-speed internet connection is essential for conducting online research, accessing cloud-based applications, and communicating with clients and colleagues. Choose a reliable internet service provider (ISP) that offers fast and stable internet connectivity with sufficient bandwidth for your business needs. Consider upgrading to a business-grade internet plan with dedicated support and enhanced security features for added reliability and performance.

6. Communication Tools: Use communication tools such as email, instant messaging, and video conferencing platforms to communicate effectively with clients, colleagues, and stakeholders. Choose communication tools that offer secure and reliable communication channels, as well as features such as file sharing, screen sharing, and group messaging for collaboration and teamwork. Popular communication tools for remote work include Microsoft Teams, Slack, Zoom, Skype, and Google Meet.

7. Backup and Security Solutions: Implement backup and security solutions to protect your accounting data and client information from loss, theft, or cyber threats. Use automated backup software or cloud backup services to regularly backup your data to an offsite location and ensure redundancy in case of hardware failure or data loss. Invest in antivirus software, firewall protection, and encryption

tools to safeguard your computer systems and networks against malware, viruses, and unauthorized access.

8. Mobile Devices: Consider using mobile devices such as smartphones and tablets to stay connected and productive while on the go. Use mobile apps for accounting software, cloud storage, and communication tools to access your business data, respond to client inquiries, and manage tasks remotely. Choose mobile devices with compatible operating systems and sufficient processing power and storage capacity to support your business applications and workflows effectively.

Ensuring Data Security and Confidentiality

Ensuring data security and confidentiality is paramount for maintaining the trust and confidence of your clients and protecting sensitive financial information. As a bookkeeping service provider, you handle confidential financial data and personal information, making it essential to implement robust security measures and protocols to safeguard against data breaches, unauthorized access, and cyber threats.

Here's a detailed overview of how to ensure data security and confidentiality in your bookkeeping service:

1. Secure Data Storage: Store financial records, client data, and sensitive information securely using encrypted storage solutions and access controls. Implement password protection, encryption, and multi-factor authentication to restrict access to confidential data and prevent unauthorized users from accessing sensitive information. Use secure cloud storage services with built-in encryption and data protection features to store and backup your data securely in the cloud.

2. Access Control: Limit access to sensitive data and financial records to authorized individuals only. Implement user permissions

and access controls to restrict access to confidential information based on roles, responsibilities, and job functions. Regularly review and update user permissions to ensure that employees and contractors have appropriate access levels to perform their duties effectively while minimizing the risk of unauthorized access or data exposure.

3. Data Encryption: Encrypt sensitive data both in transit and at rest to protect it from interception or unauthorized access. Use encryption technologies such as Secure Sockets Layer (SSL) or Transport Layer Security (TLS) to encrypt data transmitted over the internet, and encrypt stored data using encryption algorithms such as Advanced Encryption Standard (AES) to prevent unauthorized access to data stored on servers, devices, or removable media.

4. Regular Backups: Implement regular backup procedures to protect against data loss and ensure business continuity in the event of hardware failure, data corruption, or cyber-attacks. Back up your accounting data, client files, and important documents regularly to secure cloud storage or offline backup devices, and test your backup systems regularly to verify data integrity and reliability. Maintain multiple copies of backups in different locations to ensure redundancy and resilience against data loss.

5. Secure Network Infrastructure: Secure your computer systems, networks, and internet connections to prevent unauthorized access,

malware infections, and cyber-attacks. Use firewalls, intrusion detection systems, and antivirus software to protect against network threats and malicious activity. Update and patch your operating systems, software applications, and network devices regularly to address security vulnerabilities and minimize the risk of exploitation by cyber criminals.

6. Employee Training and Awareness: Train employees and contractors on data security best practices, policies, and procedures to raise awareness and promote a culture of security within your organization. Educate staff on the importance of data security, confidentiality, and compliance with privacy regulations such as the General Data Protection Regulation (GDPR) and the Health Insurance Portability and Accountability Act (HIPAA). Provide regular training sessions, security awareness programs, and phishing simulations to help employees recognize and mitigate security threats effectively.

7. Data Privacy Compliance: Comply with data privacy regulations and industry standards governing the collection, storage, and processing of personal and financial information. Familiarize yourself with applicable privacy laws such as the GDPR, HIPAA, and the California Consumer Privacy Act (CCPA), and ensure that your data handling practices align with legal requirements and regulatory guidelines. Obtain consent from clients before collecting

or processing their personal information, and implement measures to protect client confidentiality and privacy rights.

8. Incident Response Plan: Develop and implement an incident response plan to address data breaches, security incidents, and other emergencies effectively. Establish procedures for detecting, reporting, and responding to security incidents promptly, and designate responsible individuals or teams to oversee incident response efforts. Conduct regular drills and exercises to test your incident response plan and ensure that employees are prepared to respond effectively to security incidents and mitigate potential risks to data security and confidentiality.

Developing Service Offerings and Pricing

Developing service offerings and pricing for your bookkeeping service requires careful consideration of your target market, the value you provide, and the competitive landscape.

Here's a detailed overview of how to develop service offerings and pricing for your bookkeeping service:

1. Understand Client Needs: Begin by understanding the needs and preferences of your target market. Conduct market research to identify the specific pain points, challenges, and priorities of potential clients in your niche. Consider factors such as the size of businesses you want to serve, their industry sectors, and their requirements for bookkeeping and financial management services.

2. Define Your Value Proposition: Clearly articulate the value proposition of your bookkeeping service and differentiate yourself from competitors. Identify the unique benefits and advantages you offer to clients, such as expertise in a specific industry, personalized service, or advanced technology solutions. Communicate your value proposition effectively in your marketing materials, website, and client communications to attract and retain clients.

3. Design Service Offerings: Develop service offerings that align with the needs and preferences of your target market and deliver value to clients. Consider offering a range of services such as bookkeeping, payroll processing, financial reporting, tax preparation, and advisory services to meet the diverse needs of clients. Tailor your service offerings to address specific pain points or challenges faced by clients in your target market.

4. Customize Packages: Create customized service packages or tiers to cater to different client needs and budgets. Offer basic packages with essential bookkeeping services for small businesses or startups, and premium packages with additional services or features for larger enterprises or clients with more complex needs. Provide flexibility in your pricing and service offerings to accommodate variations in client requirements and preferences.

5. Set Pricing Structure: Determine your pricing structure based on the value you provide, the level of service, and the competitive landscape. Consider factors such as the complexity of the work, the time required, and the expertise involved in delivering your services. Choose a pricing model that aligns with your business goals and objectives, whether it's hourly rates, flat fees, or monthly retainers.

Be transparent and upfront about your pricing to avoid misunderstandings or disputes with clients.

6. Consider Value-Based Pricing: Consider adopting a value-based pricing approach that reflects the perceived value of your services to clients. Instead of basing your prices solely on time and effort, consider the tangible and intangible benefits clients receive from your services, such as increased efficiency, cost savings, or strategic insights. Price your services accordingly to capture the value you deliver and justify premium pricing for exceptional service quality and results.

7. Factor in Costs and Profit Margins: Take into account your costs, overhead expenses, and desired profit margins when setting your prices. Calculate your costs of delivering services, including labor, software subscriptions, office expenses, and marketing costs, and determine the minimum pricing required to cover your expenses and generate a reasonable profit. Monitor your pricing and profitability regularly and adjust your prices as needed to maintain profitability and competitiveness in the market.

8. Communicate Value to Clients: Clearly communicate the value of your services to clients and justify your pricing based on the benefits and outcomes you deliver. Highlight the expertise, experience, and qualifications of your team, as well as the quality of your services, technology solutions, and customer support. Provide testimonials, case studies, and client references to demonstrate the positive impact of your services and build trust with potential clients.

9. Offer Pricing Options: Offer pricing options and flexibility to accommodate different client budgets and preferences. Provide tiered pricing structures with different levels of service and pricing tiers, as well as customizable options to tailor services to individual client needs. Offer discounts or promotions for new clients, referrals, or bundled services to incentivize sign-ups and encourage repeat business.

10. Review and Adjust Pricing Regularly: Continuously monitor your pricing strategy and performance to ensure competitiveness and profitability. Review your pricing regularly in response to changes in market conditions, client feedback, or shifts in your business environment. Adjust your pricing as needed to reflect changes in costs, demand, or competition and maintain alignment with your business goals and objectives.

Defining Your Bookkeeping Services and Packages

Defining your bookkeeping services and packages involves outlining the specific services you offer, the scope of each service, and the pricing structure for your packages.

Here's a detailed overview of how to define your bookkeeping services and packages:

1. Identify Core Services: Begin by identifying the core bookkeeping services you offer to clients. These may include basic bookkeeping tasks such as data entry, bank reconciliations, accounts payable and receivable management, payroll processing, financial statement preparation, and tax filing support. Consider the needs and preferences of your target market and the types of businesses you want to serve when defining your core services.

2. Determine Service Scope: Define the scope of each bookkeeping service to clarify what is included and excluded in each package. Specify the frequency of tasks, the level of detail, and the deliverables provided to clients for each service. For example, specify whether bank reconciliations are performed monthly, quarterly, or annually, and whether financial statements include balance sheets, income statements, and cash flow statements.

3. Create Service Packages: Develop service packages or bundles that combine multiple bookkeeping services into cohesive offerings for clients. Consider grouping related services together based on client needs, complexity, or industry requirements. For example, create a basic package for small businesses with essential bookkeeping services such as data entry and bank reconciliations, and offer premium packages with additional services such as payroll processing, tax preparation, and financial analysis.

4. Tailor Packages to Client Needs: Customize your service packages to meet the specific needs and preferences of different client segments. Offer flexibility in your packages to accommodate variations in client requirements, industry sectors, and business sizes. Provide options for clients to add or remove services from packages based on their individual needs and budgets, and offer customizable solutions to address unique challenges or requirements.

5. Define Pricing Structure: Determine the pricing structure for your service packages based on the value you provide, the level of service, and the competitive landscape. Choose a pricing model that aligns with your business goals and objectives, whether it's hourly rates, flat fees, or monthly retainers. Consider factors such as the

complexity of the work, the time required, and the expertise involved in delivering your services when setting your prices.

6. Communicate Package Details: Clearly communicate the details of your service packages to clients to help them understand what is included and the benefits they will receive. Provide comprehensive descriptions of each service, including the tasks performed, the frequency of service delivery, and any additional features or options available. Use clear and concise language to avoid confusion and ensure transparency in your pricing and service offerings.

7. Highlight Value Proposition: Highlight the value proposition of your service packages to differentiate yourself from competitors and attract clients. Emphasize the benefits and advantages of choosing your packages, such as expertise, reliability, accuracy, and convenience. Communicate the tangible and intangible benefits clients will receive from your services, such as time savings, improved financial visibility, and peace of mind.

8. Offer Add-On Services: In addition to your standard service packages, consider offering add-on services or optional extras to provide additional value to clients and generate additional revenue. These may include services such as tax planning, financial analysis, budgeting and forecasting, or advisory services. Offer add-on services as standalone options or as enhancements to existing

packages to give clients flexibility in customizing their service plans.

9. Provide Transparent Pricing: Be transparent about your pricing and fees for service packages to build trust and credibility with clients. Clearly outline the cost of each package and any additional fees or charges associated with specific services or customizations. Provide pricing details upfront and address any questions or concerns clients may have about pricing to ensure transparency and avoid misunderstandings.

10. Review and Update Packages: Regularly review and update your service packages to ensure they remain relevant, competitive, and aligned with client needs and market trends. Monitor client feedback, industry developments, and changes in your business environment to identify opportunities for improvement or adjustments to your service offerings and pricing. Continuously iterate and refine your packages to optimize value delivery and drive business growth and profitability.

Determining Competitive Pricing Strategies

Determining competitive pricing strategies for your bookkeeping service involves balancing profitability with competitiveness in the market.

Here's a detailed overview of how to determine competitive pricing strategies:

1. Market Research: Start by conducting thorough market research to understand the pricing landscape in your industry and geographic area. Analyze the pricing strategies of competitors offering similar bookkeeping services and packages, including their pricing structure, pricing models, and value proposition. Identify pricing trends, benchmarks, and pricing ranges to inform your pricing strategy.

2. Value-Based Pricing: Consider adopting a value-based pricing approach that reflects the perceived value of your services to clients. Assess the unique benefits and advantages you offer compared to competitors and price your services accordingly. Emphasize the value and benefits clients will receive from choosing your services, such as expertise, reliability, accuracy, and personalized support,

and justify premium pricing based on the tangible and intangible benefits you provide.

3. Cost-Plus Pricing: Calculate your costs of delivering bookkeeping services, including labor, overhead expenses, software subscriptions, and other operational costs. Determine your desired profit margin and add a markup to cover your costs and generate a reasonable profit. Use cost-plus pricing as a baseline for setting your prices and adjust your pricing strategy based on market conditions, competitive factors, and client demand.

4. Competitive Benchmarking: Benchmark your pricing against competitors offering similar bookkeeping services to ensure competitiveness in the market. Compare your pricing structure, pricing levels, and pricing models with competitors to identify pricing gaps or opportunities for differentiation. Assess how your pricing compares to competitors in terms of value, quality, and service offerings, and adjust your prices as needed to remain competitive.

5. Differentiation: Differentiate your bookkeeping services and packages from competitors to justify premium pricing and stand out in the market. Highlight the unique benefits and advantages of choosing your services, such as expertise in a specific industry,

personalized service, advanced technology solutions, or additional value-added services. Communicate the tangible and intangible benefits clients will receive from your services to justify higher prices and differentiate yourself from competitors.

6. Tiered Pricing: Consider offering tiered pricing options with different levels of service and pricing tiers to appeal to a broader range of clients. Create basic packages with essential bookkeeping services at lower price points for price-sensitive clients, and offer premium packages with additional services or features at higher price points for clients willing to pay for added value. Provide flexibility in your pricing and service offerings to accommodate variations in client needs and budgets.

7. Promotional Pricing: Use promotional pricing strategies such as discounts, promotions, or special offers to attract new clients and incentivize sign-ups. Offer introductory discounts or promotional rates for new clients or first-time customers to encourage trial and adoption of your services. Run seasonal promotions, referral programs, or limited-time offers to stimulate demand and drive sales during slow periods or peak seasons.

8. Dynamic Pricing: Implement dynamic pricing strategies that adjust pricing in response to changes in market demand, client preferences, or competitive pressures. Monitor market conditions, competitor pricing, and client feedback to identify opportunities for

pricing optimization and adjust your prices accordingly. Offer flexible pricing options, negotiate pricing terms with clients, and adapt your pricing strategy in real-time to maximize revenue and profitability.

9. Customer Segmentation: Segment your target market based on factors such as industry, company size, revenue, and service requirements to tailor pricing strategies to specific client segments. Offer customized pricing plans, discounts, or incentives based on client needs, preferences, and purchasing behavior. Provide personalized pricing quotes or proposals based on individual client requirements and negotiate pricing terms to maximize value and satisfaction for both parties.

10. Continuous Monitoring and Adjustment: Continuously monitor and analyze your pricing strategy and performance to identify opportunities for optimization and improvement. Track key performance indicators (KPIs) such as revenue, profit margins, customer acquisition costs, and client retention rates to assess the effectiveness of your pricing strategy. Solicit feedback from clients, review market trends, and adjust your pricing strategy as needed to remain competitive and profitable in the market.

Offering Value-Added Services to Attract and Retain Clients

Offering value-added services is an effective strategy for attracting and retaining clients for your bookkeeping service. By providing additional services that go beyond basic bookkeeping tasks, you can differentiate yourself from competitors, enhance client satisfaction, and build long-term relationships with clients.

Here's a detailed overview of how to offer value-added services to attract and retain clients:

1. Understand Client Needs: Start by understanding the needs and preferences of your clients through regular communication, feedback sessions, and needs assessments. Identify pain points, challenges, and opportunities for improvement in their business operations, financial management, and strategic planning. Tailor your value-added services to address specific client needs and provide solutions that add measurable value to their businesses.

2. Identify Value-Added Services: Identify value-added services that complement your core bookkeeping offerings and align with client needs and industry trends. Consider offering services such as financial analysis, budgeting and forecasting, cash flow management, tax planning, business advisory, and strategic

consulting. Look for opportunities to expand your service offerings based on client feedback, market demand, and your expertise and capabilities.

3. Highlight Benefits and Outcomes: Clearly communicate the benefits and outcomes clients will receive from your value-added services to justify their investment and demonstrate the value proposition. Emphasize the tangible and intangible benefits such as cost savings, increased efficiency, improved decision-making, risk mitigation, and strategic insights. Provide case studies, testimonials, and success stories to illustrate the positive impact of your value-added services on client businesses.

4. Customize Solutions: Customize value-added services to meet the specific needs and objectives of individual clients. Offer personalized solutions tailored to their industry, business size, growth stage, and strategic goals. Conduct thorough assessments and analyses to identify areas for improvement and opportunities for value creation, and develop customized service plans and recommendations to address client needs effectively.

5. Integrate Technology Solutions: Leverage technology solutions and software tools to enhance the delivery of value-added services and streamline client workflows. Implement advanced analytics, reporting, and visualization tools to provide actionable insights and strategic recommendations to clients. Utilize cloud-based

accounting platforms, collaboration tools, and workflow automation solutions to improve efficiency, transparency, and collaboration with clients.

6. Provide Education and Training: Offer educational resources, training sessions, and workshops to empower clients with the knowledge and skills to leverage your value-added services effectively. Educate clients on financial management best practices, industry trends, regulatory changes, and emerging technologies to help them make informed decisions and optimize their business performance. Offer ongoing support and guidance to ensure clients maximize the value of your services over time.

7. Demonstrate Expertise and Thought Leadership: Position yourself as a trusted advisor and thought leader in your field by demonstrating expertise, credibility, and authority in offering value-added services. Stay abreast of industry developments, market trends, and best practices in financial management and advisory services. Share insights, thought leadership articles, and industry updates with clients to showcase your expertise and provide value-added knowledge and perspective.

8. Measure and Communicate Results: Measure the impact and effectiveness of your value-added services by tracking key performance indicators (KPIs) such as revenue growth, cost savings, profitability improvements, and client satisfaction scores. Regularly

review and analyze performance metrics to assess the ROI of your services and identify opportunities for improvement or refinement. Communicate results and success stories to clients to reinforce the value of your services and build trust and confidence in your capabilities.

9. Offer Bundled Packages: Package value-added services with your core bookkeeping offerings to create bundled service packages that provide comprehensive solutions to clients. Offer tiered pricing options with different levels of service and features to accommodate varying client needs and budgets. Provide flexibility in your packaging and pricing to allow clients to customize their service plans and select the combination of services that best meet their requirements.

10. Continuously Innovate and Evolve: Stay agile and adaptive to evolving client needs, market dynamics, and industry trends by continuously innovating and evolving your value-added service offerings. Regularly review and update your service portfolio based on client feedback, market research, and emerging opportunities. Experiment with new service offerings, technologies, and delivery models to stay competitive and meet the changing needs of your clients effectively.

Marketing and Promotion Strategies

Marketing and promotion strategies are essential for attracting new clients, increasing brand awareness, and growing your bookkeeping service business.

Here's a detailed overview of effective marketing and promotion strategies for your bookkeeping service:

1. Define Your Target Audience: Identify your target market and ideal clients based on factors such as industry, business size, location, and specific needs. Understand their pain points, challenges, and priorities to tailor your marketing messages and strategies effectively.

2. Develop a Unique Value Proposition: Clearly articulate the unique value proposition of your bookkeeping service and differentiate yourself from competitors. Highlight your expertise, reliability, accuracy, personalized service, and any unique offerings or specialization areas that set you apart in the market.

3. Build a Professional Brand: Invest in branding to create a professional and memorable identity for your bookkeeping service. Develop a cohesive brand identity, including a logo, color scheme, and visual elements that reflect your brand personality and values. Ensure consistency across all marketing materials, website, social media profiles, and communications to build brand recognition and trust.

4. Create a Professional Website: Develop a professional website that serves as a central hub for your bookkeeping service and provides essential information about your services, packages, pricing, and contact details. Optimize your website for search engines (SEO) to improve visibility and attract organic traffic from potential clients searching for bookkeeping services online.

5. Content Marketing: Produce high-quality content that demonstrates your expertise, educates your target audience, and provides value to potential clients. Create blog posts, articles, case studies, whitepapers, and guides on topics related to bookkeeping, financial management, tax compliance, and small business tips. Share your content on your website, blog, social media channels, and email newsletters to engage and attract clients.

6. Social Media Marketing: Leverage social media platforms such as LinkedIn, Facebook, Twitter, and Instagram to connect with potential clients, build relationships, and promote your bookkeeping

services. Share informative and engaging content, participate in industry discussions, and interact with followers to showcase your expertise and establish credibility in your field.

7. Networking and Referral Marketing: Build relationships with other professionals, business owners, and industry contacts through networking events, industry associations, and business networking groups. Attend local business events, seminars, and workshops to meet potential clients and referral partners. Encourage satisfied clients to refer your services to their network and offer incentives or rewards for successful referrals.

8. Online Advertising: Consider investing in online advertising channels such as Google Ads, social media ads, and display advertising to reach potential clients and drive traffic to your website. Target specific demographics, interests, and geographic locations to maximize the effectiveness of your advertising campaigns. Monitor and optimize your ad campaigns regularly to improve performance and ROI.

9. Email Marketing: Build an email list of prospects, clients, and leads and use email marketing to nurture relationships, stay top of mind, and promote your bookkeeping services. Send regular newsletters, updates, and promotional offers to your email subscribers with valuable content, industry insights, and special offers to encourage engagement and conversions.

10. Client Testimonials and Reviews: Collect client testimonials, reviews, and success stories to showcase the positive experiences and outcomes of working with your bookkeeping service. Display testimonials on your website, social media profiles, and marketing materials to build credibility, trust, and confidence in your services and attract new clients.

11. Offer Free Consultations or Workshops: Provide free consultations, workshops, or webinars to educate potential clients about the benefits of bookkeeping services and demonstrate your expertise. Offer valuable insights, tips, and advice on financial management, tax compliance, and business growth strategies to establish yourself as a trusted advisor and attract new clients.

12. Monitor and Measure Results: Track and analyze the performance of your marketing efforts using key performance indicators (KPIs) such as website traffic, leads generated, conversion rates, and client acquisition costs. Use analytics tools and metrics to evaluate the effectiveness of each marketing channel and campaign and make data-driven decisions to optimize your marketing strategy and maximize ROI.

Creating a Marketing Plan Tailored To Your Target Audience

Creating a marketing plan tailored to your target audience involves developing a comprehensive strategy to reach and engage potential clients who are most likely to benefit from your bookkeeping services.

Here's a detailed overview of how to create a marketing plan tailored to your target audience:

1. Understand Your Target Audience: Start by gaining a deep understanding of your target audience, including their demographics, preferences, needs, and pain points. Conduct market research, analyze customer data, and gather insights to identify your ideal clients and segment them based on factors such as industry, business size, location, and specific challenges or requirements.

2. Define Marketing Objectives: Set clear and specific marketing objectives aligned with your business goals and target audience. Determine what you want to achieve with your marketing efforts, whether it's increasing brand awareness, generating leads, driving website traffic, or improving client retention. Establish measurable goals and key performance indicators (KPIs) to track progress and evaluate the success of your marketing initiatives.

3. Develop a Unique Value Proposition: Craft a unique value proposition that resonates with your target audience and sets you apart from competitors. Clearly articulate the benefits and advantages of choosing your bookkeeping services, such as expertise, reliability, accuracy, personalized support, and industry specialization. Communicate your value proposition consistently across all marketing channels and touchpoints to reinforce brand messaging and differentiation.

4. Identify Marketing Channels: Identify the most effective marketing channels and platforms to reach your target audience and promote your bookkeeping services. Consider a mix of online and offline channels, including digital marketing channels such as website, search engine optimization (SEO), social media, email marketing, content marketing, and online advertising, as well as offline channels such as networking events, referrals, and local community engagement.

5. Tailor Messaging and Content: Tailor your marketing messaging and content to resonate with the specific needs, preferences, and pain points of your target audience. Develop compelling and relevant content that addresses common challenges, offers solutions, and provides value to potential clients. Customize your messaging and content based on client segments, industry sectors, and stages of the buyer's journey to ensure relevance and effectiveness.

6. Create a Content Calendar: Develop a content calendar outlining the topics, formats, and publishing schedule for your marketing content across various channels. Plan and schedule blog posts, articles, social media posts, email newsletters, webinars, and other content initiatives to maintain consistency and engagement with your target audience. Align your content calendar with key events, holidays, and industry trends to capitalize on timely opportunities and stay relevant.

7. Implement Lead Generation Strategies: Implement lead generation strategies to attract potential clients and convert them into leads for your bookkeeping services. Offer valuable resources, such as e-books, guides, checklists, or templates, in exchange for contact information through lead capture forms on your website. Use targeted advertising, landing pages, and call-to-action buttons to drive traffic to your lead capture pages and encourage sign-ups.

8. Engage and Nurture Leads: Engage and nurture leads through targeted email marketing campaigns, personalized follow-up messages, and automated workflows. Provide relevant content, educational resources, and value-added insights to nurture relationships with leads and move them through the sales funnel. Use marketing automation tools and segmentation to deliver personalized messages based on lead behavior, interests, and preferences.

9. Build Brand Awareness: Increase brand awareness and visibility among your target audience through strategic brand-building initiatives. Participate in industry events, conferences, and trade shows to showcase your expertise and network with potential clients. Collaborate with complementary businesses, influencers, or industry associations to extend your reach and amplify your brand message. Leverage social media platforms, online communities, and local media outlets to raise awareness of your bookkeeping services and establish your brand presence.

10. Measure and Optimize Performance: Monitor and measure the performance of your marketing efforts using analytics tools and metrics to evaluate the effectiveness of your marketing plan. Track key performance indicators (KPIs) such as website traffic, lead generation, conversion rates, engagement metrics, and return on investment (ROI) to assess the impact of your marketing initiatives. Analyze data, identify trends, and make data-driven decisions to optimize your marketing strategy, allocate resources effectively, and achieve your marketing objectives.

Creating a marketing plan tailored to your target audience, you can effectively reach and engage potential clients, drive awareness and interest in your bookkeeping services, and ultimately, attract and retain clients for your business. Focus on understanding your audience, delivering value, and measuring results to continuously improve your marketing efforts and achieve your business goals.

Building an Online Presence through Website and Social Media

Building an online presence through a website and social media is a multifaceted process that requires a strategic approach to effectively showcase your brand, engage with your audience, and ultimately drive growth. The journey begins with the creation of a professional website, your digital storefront, where you can convey your brand's message, values, and offerings in a clear and engaging manner. This platform serves as the cornerstone of your digital identity, providing a space where customers can learn about your products or services, contact you, and even make purchases directly.

When designing your website, it's essential to focus on user experience, ensuring the site is easy to navigate, aesthetically pleasing, and mobile-friendly, as a significant portion of web traffic now comes from mobile devices. Incorporating search engine optimization (SEO) techniques from the outset is crucial to improve your site's visibility in search engine results, making it easier for potential customers to find you among the vast digital landscape.

Parallel to website development, establishing a strong social media presence is equally important. Social media platforms offer a unique opportunity to connect with your audience in a more personal and direct way. The key is to identify which platforms your target audience frequents the most, whether it's Instagram, Facebook, Twitter, LinkedIn, or others, and establish a consistent presence there.

Content is king in the digital realm, so creating engaging, informative, and shareable content is vital. This could range from blog posts and videos to infographics and live streams, depending on the platform and what resonates best with your audience. The goal is to provide value to your followers, whether through insights, entertainment, or solutions to their problems, which in turn can foster trust and loyalty towards your brand.

Interaction is another critical aspect of building an online presence. This means not just posting content, but also actively engaging with your audience by responding to comments, messages, and reviews, participating in conversations, and even reaching out to other users and brands for collaborations. This two-way communication helps build a community around your brand, driving engagement and increasing visibility.

Analytics play a crucial role throughout this process, offering insights into what's working and what isn't. By monitoring the performance of your website and social media accounts, you can understand your audience's behavior and preferences, enabling you to refine your strategies, improve user experience, and tailor your content to better meet their needs.

Consistency is the thread that ties all these elements together. Maintaining a consistent brand voice and visual identity across your website and social media platforms helps reinforce your brand image and makes your business more recognizable. Likewise, regular updates and consistent engagement are essential to keep your audience interested and engaged.

Building an online presence through a website and social media is an ongoing endeavor that combines strategic planning, creative content creation, active engagement, and continuous analysis and adjustment. It's about creating a digital ecosystem where your brand can thrive, connect with and expand your audience, and drive your business forward in the digital age.

Networking and Collaborating With Other Professionals and Businesses

Networking and collaborating with other professionals and businesses is a dynamic and invaluable strategy for growth, innovation, and establishing a robust presence within your industry. It begins with the proactive pursuit of relationships that offer mutual benefit, grounded in the understanding that success in any field is often a collective effort. Engaging with peers, mentors, and complementary businesses opens doors to new opportunities, shared knowledge, and enhanced visibility.

The foundation of effective networking is building genuine relationships rather than merely seeking immediate gains. This involves attending industry events, conferences, and workshops where you can meet like-minded professionals. It's not just about exchanging business cards but about engaging in meaningful conversations, showing genuine interest in others' work, and exploring how you can support each other's goals. Social media platforms, particularly LinkedIn, provide another powerful tool for connecting with peers, joining professional groups, and participating in discussions relevant to your field.

Collaborating with other businesses and professionals can take various forms, from co-hosting events and webinars to engaging in joint projects or offering complementary services. Such partnerships can significantly amplify your reach, allowing you to tap into each other's networks and customer bases. Collaborations also enable you to leverage diverse skill sets and perspectives, potentially leading to innovative solutions and offerings that can set you apart in the market.

The key to successful collaborations is clear communication and alignment on goals, expectations, and contributions from the outset. Whether it's a formal partnership or a more casual project-based collaboration, defining these elements helps ensure that all parties are working towards a common objective and that the collaboration is mutually beneficial. Building a strong network also involves being a valuable resource to others. This could mean sharing opportunities, offering advice, or connecting people within your network with each other. By being generous with your knowledge and resources, you establish yourself as a respected and reliable member of your professional community, which can lead to more opportunities coming your way.

Regularly engaging with your network is crucial to keeping relationships vibrant and top-of-mind. This can be as simple as checking in via email, sharing relevant articles or resources, or meeting for coffee. The goal is to maintain a connection, so when opportunities for collaboration arise, you're already in a position to act.

The benefits of networking and collaborating extend beyond business growth; they also include personal development. Interacting with a diverse group of professionals exposes you to new ideas, insights, and approaches, challenging you to think differently and improve your skills. It's a continual learning process that can make you more adaptable, innovative, and effective in your career.

Networking and collaborating with other professionals and businesses is a strategic approach to building a thriving professional ecosystem. It's about creating value through relationships, exploring new avenues for growth, and fostering a culture of cooperation and innovation. As the business landscape becomes increasingly interconnected, the ability to network and collaborate effectively has never been more critical to achieving long-term success and making a meaningful impact in your industry.

Client Acquisition and Relationship Management

Client acquisition and relationship management are essential processes that ensure the steady growth and sustainability of a business by attracting new clients and maintaining strong, lasting relationships with existing ones. These processes require a strategic approach that combines understanding your market, effective communication, and providing exceptional value to your clients.

The journey often begins with identifying your target audience, understanding their needs, challenges, and preferences. This knowledge allows you to tailor your marketing and outreach efforts to attract the clients most likely to benefit from your services or products. Techniques such as content marketing, social media engagement, and email marketing campaigns can be instrumental in drawing attention to your brand. Moreover, leveraging search engine optimization (SEO) and pay-per-click (PPC) advertising can significantly increase your visibility to potential clients actively searching for solutions that you offer.

Once potential clients are aware of your business, converting them into actual clients involves clear communication of the value your services or products provide. This is where personalized engagement strategies come into play. Whether through direct outreach, personalized emails, or targeted social media campaigns, the goal is to demonstrate how your offerings align with their specific needs or solve their particular problems.

However, acquiring a new client is just the beginning. The long-term success of a business often relies on its ability to manage relationships with its clients effectively. This involves not only consistently meeting or exceeding client expectations but also maintaining open lines of communication. Regular check-ins, updates on new services or products, and asking for feedback are all practices that can enhance client satisfaction and loyalty. Client relationship management also extends to how you handle challenges or complaints. Being proactive, responsive, and solution-oriented in the face of problems can turn potentially negative experiences into opportunities to demonstrate your commitment to client satisfaction. This not only helps in retaining clients but can also lead to referrals, as clients who feel valued and well-served are more likely to recommend your business to others.

In addition to these direct approaches, creating a sense of community around your brand can further strengthen client relationships. Hosting events, workshops, or webinars provides an opportunity for clients to engage with your brand and with each other, fostering a sense of belonging and loyalty. Technology plays a crucial role in facilitating client acquisition and relationship management. Customer Relationship Management (CRM) systems can help businesses track interactions with potential and current clients, manage leads, and streamline communication. These systems can also provide valuable insights into client behavior, preferences, and satisfaction, enabling businesses to tailor their strategies more effectively.

Strategies for Finding and Acquiring Clients

Finding and acquiring clients is a fundamental aspect of business growth and sustainability. It involves a multi-faceted approach that leverages both digital and traditional strategies tailored to the unique needs and behaviors of your target audience. Understanding your market, delivering value, and building relationships are at the heart of effective client acquisition.

At the core of finding clients is the need to understand who they are, what they need, and where you can find them. This understanding forms the foundation of your marketing and outreach efforts. Research and market analysis play crucial roles here, enabling you to identify the demographics, preferences, and behaviors of your potential clients. Armed with this knowledge, you can craft targeted messages and choose the most effective channels for communication.

In the digital age, an online presence is indispensable for reaching potential clients. A well-designed website that clearly communicates what you offer, its value, and how clients can engage with your services or products is vital. Search Engine Optimization (SEO) enhances your visibility by ensuring that your website ranks well in relevant search engine results, making it easier for potential clients to find you. Additionally, content marketing through blogs, videos, and other forms of content can establish your expertise, increase your reach, and attract clients by providing them with valuable information related to their needs and interests.

Social media platforms offer another powerful channel for engaging with potential clients. By identifying the platforms where your target audience is most active, you can engage in conversations, share relevant content, and build a community around your brand. Paid advertising on these platforms can also be a highly effective tool for reaching a broader audience with precision targeting based on demographics, interests, and behaviors.

Networking and referrals are time-tested strategies for client acquisition that complement digital efforts. Building relationships with other professionals and businesses in your industry can lead to opportunities for collaboration and referrals. Similarly, encouraging satisfied clients to refer others to your business can be a highly effective way to gain new clients, as recommendations from trusted sources are often seen as more credible and persuasive.

Participating in industry events, conferences, and trade shows can also be a valuable strategy for meeting potential clients. These events provide opportunities to present your offerings, connect with potential clients face-to-face, and establish your presence in the industry.

Cold outreach, such as cold emailing or calling, can be challenging but rewarding when done correctly. Personalizing your messages, demonstrating an understanding of the recipient's needs, and clearly articulating how you can provide value can increase your chances of success.

In all these efforts, the key is to communicate effectively, demonstrating the value you provide and differentiating yourself from competitors. Building trust and relationships is central to converting potential leads into clients. This requires consistency, patience, and a focus on providing exceptional service and value.

Finally, leveraging technology can streamline the client acquisition process. Customer Relationship Management (CRM) tools can help you manage leads, track interactions, and analyze the effectiveness of your strategies. Analytics tools can provide insights into the behavior of visitors to your website and the performance of your marketing campaigns, allowing you to refine your strategies over time.

Acquiring clients requires a strategic blend of understanding your market, leveraging digital and traditional marketing strategies, building relationships, and continuously evaluating and refining your approach based on feedback and performance. By focusing on delivering value and building trust, businesses can attract and retain clients in a competitive marketplace.

Building Strong Client Relationships and Trust

Building strong client relationships and trust is a nuanced art that lies at the heart of successful businesses, involving much more than just delivering a product or service. It's about creating a foundation of reliability, understanding, and mutual respect that fosters long-term partnerships rather than mere transactions. This process begins from the very first interaction and extends through the entire lifecycle of the client relationship.

Understanding your clients' needs, goals, and challenges is the first step in building this foundation. This requires active listening and empathy, showing that you're not just interested in making a sale but are genuinely invested in providing solutions that add value to their lives or businesses. By aligning your offerings closely with what your clients truly need, you demonstrate an understanding of their unique contexts, which is a cornerstone of trust. Communication is another critical element in building strong client relationships. This doesn't just mean keeping clients informed about project statuses or deliverables but also involves transparently sharing both successes and challenges. Regular, open communication helps to manage expectations and builds trust over time, as clients feel more secure when they're kept in the loop and can see that you're committed to transparency, even when things don't go as planned.

Personalization plays a crucial role in deepening client relationships. This means going beyond the one-size-fits-all approach to tailor your communication, solutions, and interactions to fit the specific needs and preferences of each client. Personalization shows that you view and value each client as an individual, which can significantly enhance their loyalty and trust in your business.

Building trust also requires reliability. Consistently meeting deadlines, keeping promises, and maintaining high-quality standards in your work are non-negotiable aspects of a trustworthy relationship. Clients need to know they can count on you to deliver what you've promised, as your reliability directly impacts their success and satisfaction.

Moreover, showing appreciation for your clients reinforces the value you place on the relationship. Small gestures like thank-you notes, personalized gifts, or even exclusive offers can make clients feel valued and deepen their connection to your brand.

Handling feedback and complaints effectively is another vital aspect of building trust. Viewing negative feedback as an opportunity to improve and promptly addressing any issues demonstrates your commitment to client satisfaction and your willingness to go the extra mile to rectify problems. This responsiveness can turn potentially negative experiences into powerful moments of trust-building.

Fostering a collaborative environment where clients feel like partners in the process rather than passive recipients can significantly strengthen the relationship. Inviting feedback, suggestions, and even criticisms shows that you value their input and are willing to adapt to better meet their needs. Collaboration like this not only leads to better outcomes but also engenders a sense of shared ownership and trust in the success of the endeavors you undertake together.

Building strong client relationships and trust is about consistently demonstrating your commitment to their success, being transparent and communicative, and treating each client as a valued partner. It's a comprehensive approach that, when executed with care and sincerity, can lead to lasting business relationships that are as rewarding personally as they are professionally.

Managing Client Expectations and Communication Effectively

Managing client expectations and communication effectively is crucial in establishing and maintaining successful business relationships. This involves a delicate balance of clarity, transparency, and ongoing dialogue to ensure both parties are aligned from the outset and remain so throughout their engagement.

The foundation of managing expectations starts with clear communication. From the very first interaction, it's essential to articulate what your services or products can and cannot do. This means providing detailed descriptions, setting realistic timelines, and being upfront about costs. Establishing these parameters early helps prevent misunderstandings and sets a clear framework for the relationship moving forward.

Effective communication also requires active listening. Paying close attention to what clients say—and what they might not say explicitly—can give you invaluable insights into their true expectations, concerns, and underlying needs. This deeper understanding allows you to tailor your approach and offerings to better meet their requirements, enhancing satisfaction and trust.

Transparency throughout the project lifecycle or the duration of the service is another key element. Keeping clients informed about progress, potential challenges, and any changes that arise helps manage their expectations in real-time. Regular updates, whether through meetings, reports, or informal check-ins, should be part of your standard communication strategy. These interactions provide opportunities to adjust expectations as needed and to reaffirm your commitment to their goals.

Another aspect of managing expectations is setting boundaries. Clearly define what is included in your services, your availability for communication, and the processes for requesting changes or additional work. Boundaries help prevent scope creep and ensure that both you and your client have a mutual understanding of the terms of engagement.

Empathy plays a significant role in effective communication and managing expectations. Recognizing and acknowledging your clients' concerns or frustrations, even when you cannot fully accommodate their requests, can go a long way in maintaining a positive relationship. Demonstrating that you understand their perspective and are working in their best interest helps to build trust and goodwill.

When unexpected issues arise—as they inevitably will—how you handle these situations can significantly impact client satisfaction and your relationship. Being proactive in addressing problems, offering solutions, and, if necessary, admitting mistakes, underscores your integrity and commitment to your clients' success.

Soliciting and acting on feedback is essential for continuous improvement and managing expectations. Encourage clients to share their thoughts on your work together, including what they believe went well and areas for improvement. This feedback loop not only helps you refine your offerings and approach but also reinforces to clients that their opinions are valued and taken seriously.

Managing client expectations and communication effectively is an ongoing process that requires clarity, transparency, and responsiveness. By establishing realistic expectations, maintaining open lines of communication, and demonstrating a genuine commitment to your clients' success, you can build strong, lasting relationships that are beneficial for all involved.

Bookkeeping Processes and Best Practices

Effective bookkeeping is crucial for the success and financial health of any business. It involves the systematic recording, organizing, and managing of financial transactions, enabling business owners to understand their financial position, make informed decisions, and ensure compliance with legal obligations. Implementing best practices in bookkeeping can streamline processes, improve accuracy, and enhance financial reporting.

Here's an overview of key bookkeeping processes and best practices:

1. Systematic Organization: A cornerstone of effective bookkeeping is the systematic organization of financial documents and records. This includes invoices, receipts, bank statements, and payroll records. Utilizing a digital filing system can enhance accessibility and security, ensuring that documents are easily retrievable and well-protected against loss or damage.

2. Use of Accounting Software: Leveraging modern accounting software can significantly improve the efficiency and accuracy of bookkeeping processes. These tools automate many aspects of bookkeeping, from transaction recording to generating financial

reports. They also minimize human error, provide real-time financial insights, and facilitate secure data storage and backup.

3. Regular Reconciliation: Regularly reconciling bank accounts and financial statements is critical to ensuring accuracy in bookkeeping. This process involves comparing internal records with bank statements to identify discrepancies and make necessary adjustments. Monthly reconciliation is recommended to catch errors early and maintain accurate financial records.

4. Accurate Expense Tracking: Keeping meticulous records of all business expenses is essential for managing cash flow, budgeting, and tax preparation. It's important to categorize expenses accurately and keep detailed records to support deductions and facilitate financial analysis.

5. Timely Invoicing and Follow-Up: Efficient invoicing and prompt follow-up on outstanding payments are vital for maintaining healthy cash flow. Establishing a regular invoicing schedule and utilizing automated reminders can help ensure timely payments from clients.

6. Compliance with Legal Requirements: Bookkeeping isn't just a financial necessity; it's also a legal requirement. Businesses must comply with tax laws, including the timely submission of tax returns and payments. Keeping accurate and comprehensive records is

essential for compliance and can protect against legal and financial penalties.

7. Regular Financial Review: Periodic reviews of financial statements, including the balance sheet, income statement, and cash flow statement, offer valuable insights into a business's financial health. These reviews can identify trends, inform decision-making, and highlight areas requiring attention or adjustment.

8. Planning for Taxes: Effective tax planning is an integral part of bookkeeping. This includes setting aside funds for tax liabilities, taking advantage of allowable deductions and credits, and maintaining detailed records to support tax filings. Consulting with a tax professional can provide guidance tailored to your business's specific needs and obligations.

9. Continuous Learning and Adaptation: The financial landscape and regulatory environment are constantly evolving. Staying informed about changes in tax laws, accounting standards, and best practices is crucial for maintaining effective bookkeeping processes.

10. Seeking Professional Assistance: While small businesses may handle bookkeeping internally during the early stages, consulting with a professional accountant or bookkeeper can provide expertise and insights that enhance financial management. Professionals can

offer strategic advice, ensure compliance, and identify opportunities for financial optimization.

Establishing Efficient Bookkeeping Processes and Workflows

Establishing efficient bookkeeping processes and workflows is a vital undertaking for any business, aiming to streamline financial operations, ensure accuracy in reporting, and facilitate informed decision-making. At the heart of efficient bookkeeping lies the adoption of a systematic approach that integrates technology, clear procedures, and regular review mechanisms to manage financial transactions and reporting with precision and transparency.

The journey towards efficiency begins with the selection of the right bookkeeping system that matches the business's size, complexity, and industry requirements. Whether it's a simple spreadsheet for a small enterprise or sophisticated accounting software for a larger operation, the choice should enable seamless recording, tracking, and analysis of financial data. Modern accounting software, offering automation for repetitive tasks such as transaction recording and invoice generation, not only saves time but also reduces the risk of human error.

Central to improving bookkeeping efficiency is the organization of financial documents. This involves setting up a consistent system for collecting, filing, and storing receipts, invoices, bank statements, and other financial documents, either digitally or physically. A well-organized system simplifies the retrieval of information, making it easier to prepare financial statements, undergo audits, and comply with tax obligations.

Implementing regular reconciliation processes is another cornerstone of efficient bookkeeping. By routinely comparing internal financial records against bank statements, businesses can identify discrepancies early, ensuring that their financial records accurately reflect actual transactions. This practice is crucial for maintaining the integrity of financial reporting and supporting effective cash flow management. Categorization of expenses and income is also essential for efficient bookkeeping. Establishing clear categories for income and expenditures not only facilitates more straightforward accounting but also aids in the analysis of financial performance, budgeting, and tax preparation. Proper categorization helps in understanding where the business is generating revenue and incurring costs, enabling more strategic financial planning.

Efficient bookkeeping also demands a proactive approach to receivables and payables management. Setting up systems for timely invoicing, tracking outstanding payments, and managing bills ensures that the business maintains healthy cash flow. Automated reminders for payments can be particularly effective, reducing the time spent on following up on late payments and helping to secure the business's financial health.

Periodic financial reviews are integral to maintaining efficiency in bookkeeping workflows. Regular analysis of financial statements allows businesses to assess their financial health, identify trends, and make informed decisions. These reviews can spotlight areas for cost reduction, opportunities for revenue enhancement, and strategies for financial optimization.

Tax planning and preparation, seamlessly integrated into bookkeeping workflows, can significantly reduce the workload and stress associated with tax seasons. By consistently recording transactions in a tax-compliant manner and maintaining organized records, businesses can streamline the tax filing process, minimize liabilities, and maximize potential deductions.

Fostering a culture of continuous improvement and adaptation in bookkeeping practices ensures that businesses remain responsive to changes in financial regulations, technology advancements, and internal growth dynamics. Regular training for staff, exploring new bookkeeping technologies, and seeking feedback from financial audits can highlight areas for further efficiency gains.

Establishing efficient bookkeeping processes and workflows involves a blend of strategic planning, technology integration, and consistent execution. By prioritizing accuracy, organization, and proactive financial management, businesses can achieve not only compliance and transparency but also a robust foundation for sustained growth and success.

Using accounting software effectively

Using accounting software effectively is pivotal for managing a business's financial health, ensuring accuracy, and streamlining accounting processes. The right software can transform the complex, time-consuming task of managing finances into a more manageable, efficient process. At the core, effective use of accounting software involves selecting a program that aligns with your business needs, setting it up correctly, and leveraging its features to optimize your accounting workflows.

Selecting the right accounting software starts with a clear understanding of your business's specific needs. Consider factors such as the size of your business, industry-specific requirements, scalability, and the complexity of your financial transactions. Many software options offer a range of features, from basic bookkeeping functionalities like invoicing and expense tracking to more advanced features such as payroll management, inventory tracking, and financial reporting. Some software also offers integration with other business tools, such as CRM systems, e-commerce platforms, and bank accounts, providing a more holistic view of your business finances.

Once you've selected a software, the initial setup is critical. This step often involves inputting detailed information about your business, including bank accounts, financial structures, tax information, and any existing financial data. Accurate setup ensures that the software can effectively manage your financial processes and generate accurate reports. Taking the time to familiarize yourself with the software's interface and features during this phase is essential. Many software providers offer tutorials, webinars, and customer support to help new users.

Regular data entry is the heartbeat of effective accounting software use. Consistently entering transactions, expenses, and income ensures that your financial information is up-to-date and accurate. This consistent data flow is crucial for real-time financial analysis and decision-making. Automation features within accounting software, such as bank feeds that automatically import transactions, can significantly reduce manual data entry and minimize errors.

Leveraging the reporting capabilities of accounting software is another key aspect of effective use. These systems can generate a variety of financial reports, such as profit and loss statements, balance sheets, and cash flow statements, with just a few clicks. Regularly reviewing these reports can provide insights into your business's financial health, identify trends, and inform strategic decisions.

Customization is a powerful feature of many accounting software options. Customizing the software to match your business's specific accounting practices, such as custom invoice templates, specific account names, or unique reporting categories, can enhance efficiency and relevance. Additionally, setting up alerts for important dates like tax submissions or invoice due dates can help ensure critical financial tasks are not overlooked.

Integrations with other business tools amplify the effectiveness of accounting software. Integrating your accounting system with tools like payroll services, payment processors, and e-commerce platforms can automate data flow across systems, reducing manual entry and providing a more comprehensive view of your finances. Regularly updating the software and backing up data are critical practices to protect your financial information and ensure compliance with the latest financial regulations and tax laws. Software updates often include new features, security enhancements, and bug fixes, which can improve functionality and safety.

With the most user-friendly accounting software, there's a learning curve and a need for financial knowledge. Investing in training for yourself or your team can maximize the benefits of the software. For complex financial situations or strategic financial planning, consulting with an accounting professional can complement the use of software, ensuring that your business's finances are well-managed and aligned with your overall business strategy.

Effectively using accounting software is a dynamic process that encompasses choosing the right software, setting it up correctly, maintaining regular data entry, leveraging reporting and customization features, integrating with other business tools, and ensuring data safety and compliance through updates and backups. With these practices, businesses can enhance their financial management, gain valuable insights, and support their overall success.

Ensuring Accuracy and Compliance with Accounting Standards

Ensuring accuracy and compliance with accounting standards is fundamental to the integrity and success of any business's financial management. This practice not only helps in presenting a true and fair view of the company's financial health but also safeguards against legal and reputational risks. To achieve this, businesses must adhere to a meticulous approach that encompasses understanding and implementing relevant accounting standards, conducting regular audits, and fostering a culture of accuracy and diligence within the organization.

Understanding and implementing the relevant accounting standards, such as Generally Accepted Accounting Principles (GAAP) in the United States or International Financial Reporting Standards (IFRS) globally, is the first step. These standards provide a framework for accounting practices and financial reporting, ensuring consistency, reliability, and comparability of financial statements. Businesses must stay updated on any changes or updates to these standards to ensure ongoing compliance.

Adopting a detail-oriented approach to recording financial transactions is crucial. Every transaction, no matter how small, should be recorded accurately and classified correctly according to the appropriate accounting standards. This requires a comprehensive understanding of the nature of each transaction and its correct accounting treatment, ensuring that the financial statements accurately reflect the company's financial status.

Regular internal audits and reviews are vital components in ensuring accuracy and compliance. These processes involve examining financial records and transactions to verify their accuracy, identify discrepancies, and ensure compliance with accounting standards and legal requirements. Regular audits help in early detection of errors or irregularities, allowing for timely corrections and adjustments.

Implementing robust internal controls is another critical aspect. Internal controls are procedures and policies designed to safeguard assets, prevent fraud, and ensure the reliability of financial reporting. This includes controls over financial reporting, authorization of transactions, and safeguarding of assets. Effective internal controls not only help in ensuring accuracy and compliance but also enhance operational efficiency.

Training and development of staff play a significant role in maintaining accuracy and compliance. Employees involved in financial management and reporting should receive regular training on relevant accounting standards, internal controls, and best practices. This ensures that they are equipped with the necessary knowledge and skills to carry out their responsibilities effectively.

Leveraging technology and accounting software can also contribute significantly to ensuring accuracy and compliance. Modern accounting software is designed to comply with current accounting standards, automate complex calculations, and reduce the risk of human error. However, it's important to ensure that the software is regularly updated and correctly configured to reflect the latest accounting standards and tax laws.

Collaboration with external auditors or accounting professionals can provide additional assurance. External auditors review the company's financial statements and internal controls, providing an independent assessment of compliance with accounting standards and the accuracy of financial reporting. Their findings can offer valuable insights and recommendations for improvement. Ensuring accuracy and compliance with accounting standards requires a multifaceted approach that includes understanding and implementing relevant standards, adopting a detail-oriented approach to transaction recording, conducting regular audits, implementing strong internal controls, investing in staff training, leveraging technology, and seeking external assurance. This comprehensive approach not only fulfills legal and regulatory obligations but also builds trust with stakeholders, including investors, creditors, and customers, thereby supporting the long-term success of the business.

Managing Finances and Cash Flow

Managing finances and cash flow is a critical aspect of running a business, as it directly influences the ability to operate, invest, and grow. Effective management of these areas requires a strategic approach that encompasses monitoring, analyzing, and planning to ensure that the business remains solvent and profitable. At the core of this process is the understanding that cash flow—the inflow and outflow of cash—is the lifeblood of any business, dictating its ability to meet its financial obligations and pursue opportunities for expansion.

One of the first steps in managing finances and cash flow is to establish a comprehensive budget that outlines expected revenues, costs, and expenses. This budget serves as a financial blueprint for the business, providing a framework for decision-making and a benchmark for measuring financial performance. By comparing actual financial results with the budget, businesses can identify variances, understand their causes, and take corrective actions to steer the business back on course.

Effective cash flow management also involves diligent tracking of cash inflows and outflows. This includes monitoring sales and collections, managing payment terms with customers and suppliers, and controlling overheads and operating expenses. Timely invoicing and follow-up on receivables are crucial to ensuring that cash inflows occur as planned. Similarly, negotiating favorable payment terms with suppliers can help delay cash outflows, improving the company's cash position. Another critical strategy is to maintain a cash reserve or emergency fund. This fund acts as a financial buffer, enabling the business to weather periods of reduced cash flow or unexpected expenses. The size of this reserve will vary depending on the nature of the business and its financial stability but having this reserve can be the difference between navigating through tough times and facing financial distress.

Leveraging technology can significantly enhance finance and cash flow management. Accounting and financial management software can automate many aspects of financial tracking and reporting, providing real-time visibility into the company's financial health. These tools can help identify trends, generate forecasts, and facilitate scenario planning, allowing businesses to make informed decisions quickly.

Effective cash flow management also requires a proactive approach to managing debt and financing. This involves choosing the right mix of debt and equity financing to fund operations and growth while ensuring that the cost of capital is minimized. It's also important to regularly review and renegotiate terms of existing debts to take advantage of lower interest rates or more favorable conditions. Strategic investment in growth opportunities is another key aspect of managing finances and cash flow. This requires a careful assessment of potential investments, considering both their expected returns and their impact on cash flow. Prioritizing investments that offer the most significant potential for growth and profitability can help ensure that limited resources are used effectively.

Setting Up Financial Systems for Your Own Business

Setting up financial systems for your business is a foundational step that can dictate the efficiency, clarity, and compliance of your operations. A well-structured financial system serves as the backbone of your business's economic activities, allowing you to track performance, manage cash flow, and make informed decisions. The process involves several key components, including selecting the right accounting software, establishing bookkeeping practices, managing invoices and payments, planning for taxes, and ensuring compliance with financial regulations.

The first step in setting up your financial system is choosing accounting software that aligns with your business needs. The market offers a variety of options, from simple bookkeeping tools for small businesses to complex accounting systems for larger enterprises. The right software should offer scalability, user-friendliness, and compatibility with other tools or platforms you use, such as payment processing or payroll services. It should also provide features necessary for your specific industry, such as inventory management for retail businesses or project billing for service-based companies.

Once you've selected your accounting software, establishing solid bookkeeping practices is essential. This involves setting up your chart of accounts, which categorizes all your business transactions into distinct accounts. A well-organized chart of accounts provides clarity and makes it easier to track income, expenses, assets, liabilities, and equity. Regularly updating and reconciling your books ensures that your financial records accurately reflect your business's operations and aids in detecting any discrepancies early.

Managing invoices and payments efficiently is crucial for maintaining healthy cash flow. This includes setting up processes for issuing invoices promptly, tracking receivables, and following up on overdue payments. On the expenses side, scheduling bill payments to avoid late fees while taking advantage of any available credit terms can optimize your cash flow. Additionally, implementing a system for expense tracking and approval can help you monitor spending and prevent budget overruns.

Tax planning is another critical aspect of your financial system. Understanding the tax obligations specific to your business type and industry is crucial. This might involve sales tax, income tax, payroll tax, and other applicable taxes. Setting aside money in a separate account for tax liabilities can prevent cash flow problems when taxes are due. Additionally, keeping abreast of tax deductions and credits you're eligible for can significantly reduce your tax burden. Consulting with a tax professional can provide valuable insights and ensure that you're maximizing tax-saving opportunities while remaining compliant with tax laws. Ensuring compliance with financial regulations and standards is paramount. This includes adhering to accounting standards, tax laws, and any industry-specific financial regulations. Non-compliance can result in legal penalties and damage to your business's reputation. Staying informed about changes in financial regulations and seeking expert advice when necessary can help you navigate these complexities.

Managing Cash Flow and Expenses Effectively

Managing cash flow and expenses effectively is crucial for the financial health and sustainability of any business. This involves monitoring and optimizing the movement of money into and out of your business, ensuring that you always have sufficient funds available to cover your obligations. Effective management of cash flow and expenses requires a proactive approach, focusing on accurate forecasting, prudent spending, and strategic financial planning.

At the core of managing cash flow is the ability to accurately predict your business's financial inflows and outflows over a certain period. This forecasting enables you to anticipate periods of cash surplus or shortage, allowing for timely adjustments in your financial strategy. To achieve accurate forecasts, you should analyze historical financial data, consider seasonal variations in your business, and account for external factors that could impact your revenue or expenses.

Expense management is another critical component. This involves not just tracking and recording every financial transaction but also evaluating your expenses to identify areas where you can reduce costs without compromising the quality of your product or service.

Regularly reviewing your expenses can help you spot trends, such as rising costs in certain areas, enabling you to negotiate better terms with suppliers or find more cost-effective alternatives.

One effective strategy for managing cash flow is to align your receivables and payables. This means encouraging faster payments from your customers while seeking favorable credit terms from your suppliers. Offering discounts for early payments can incentivize customers to pay sooner, improving your cash inflow. Conversely, negotiating longer payment terms with suppliers can extend your cash outflow period, improving your cash on hand.

Another key practice is maintaining a cash reserve. A cash reserve acts as a financial buffer that can help you navigate through periods of low cash flow without having to resort to emergency funding options, which might be costly. The size of this reserve will depend on the nature of your business and the variability of your cash flow.

Leveraging technology can greatly enhance your cash flow and expense management. Accounting software and financial management tools can automate the tracking of cash flow and expenses, provide real-time financial insights, and simplify financial forecasting. Many of these tools also offer features like invoice management and automatic payment reminders, which can help in managing receivables and payables more efficiently.

Regular communication with stakeholders, including employees, suppliers, and financial institutions, is essential. For instance, keeping your bank informed about your financial status and future funding needs can facilitate easier access to credit when needed. Similarly, transparent communication with suppliers about your payment capabilities can foster better relationships and more favorable payment terms. In managing expenses, it's important to differentiate between essential and non-essential spending, especially in times of financial constraint. Investment in areas that contribute directly to revenue generation should be prioritized, while discretionary spending should be carefully evaluated.

Continuous learning and adaptation are vital. The financial landscape is constantly evolving, and so are the challenges and opportunities for managing cash flow and expenses. Staying informed about best practices, regulatory changes, and emerging financial management technologies can provide you with new strategies for optimizing your business's financial health. Managing cash flow and expenses effectively requires a combination of accurate financial forecasting, prudent expense management, strategic alignment of receivables and payables, maintaining a cash reserve, leveraging technology, clear communication with stakeholders, and a commitment to continuous improvement. By adopting these strategies, businesses can ensure they have the financial agility to support their operations and growth objectives.

Budgeting and Forecasting For Long-Term Sustainability

Budgeting and forecasting are critical financial management practices that pave the way for the long-term sustainability of any business. These processes involve creating detailed plans for your financial future, allowing you to set financial goals, anticipate potential challenges, and make informed decisions. While budgeting focuses on creating a plan for your income and expenses over a specific period, forecasting extends this view into the future, helping you predict financial trends and outcomes based on historical data and market analysis.

Effective budgeting starts with a comprehensive understanding of your current financial situation. This means analyzing past income statements, balance sheets, and cash flow statements to gain insights into your revenue streams, fixed and variable expenses, and cash flow patterns. With this information, you can set realistic financial goals that align with your business's strategic objectives, such as expanding into new markets, launching new products, or increasing operational efficiency. The next step involves estimating future income and expenses. This requires a detailed analysis of market conditions, sales forecasts, pricing strategies, and cost structures. It's important to account for both fixed costs, such as rent and salaries, and variable costs, which may fluctuate based on production levels or market demand. Additionally, setting aside funds for unexpected expenses or economic downturns can provide a financial cushion, ensuring that your business remains resilient in the face of unforeseen challenges.

Once you have a clear picture of your anticipated income and expenses, you can create a budget that outlines how your resources will be allocated to achieve your financial goals. Regularly reviewing and adjusting this budget in response to actual financial performance or changes in market conditions is crucial. This iterative process ensures that your budget remains relevant and effective in guiding your financial decisions. Forecasting, on the other hand, extends beyond the immediate budgeting period and looks into the longer-term financial future of your business. By analyzing trends in your financial data and considering external factors such as economic conditions, industry trends, and competitive dynamics, you can develop financial forecasts that provide insights into potential revenue growth, profitability, and cash flow trajectories.

Effective forecasting enables you to anticipate changes in your business environment and adapt your strategies accordingly. For example, if your forecast indicates a potential cash flow shortfall, you can take proactive measures such as securing financing, cutting unnecessary expenses, or adjusting your sales strategy to mitigate the impact.

Both budgeting and forecasting require a commitment to accuracy, detail, and flexibility. Utilizing accounting software and financial modeling tools can enhance the precision of your budgets and forecasts by providing robust data analysis and scenario planning capabilities. These tools can help you test different assumptions and evaluate the potential financial impact of various strategic decisions, allowing you to navigate your business towards its long-term goals with greater confidence.

In addition to leveraging technology, engaging with stakeholders throughout the budgeting and forecasting process is key. Input from department heads, financial advisors, and other key personnel can provide valuable insights and ensure that your financial plans are aligned with operational capabilities and strategic objectives.

Scaling Your Business

Scaling your business involves expanding its capacity and revenue while maintaining or improving operational efficiency and profitability. It's a critical phase in a business's lifecycle, requiring strategic planning, resource optimization, and often, a shift in mindset. Successfully scaling a business means growing in a way that is sustainable and manageable, ensuring that the quality of your product or service remains high even as you reach more customers.

To start, a clear understanding of your business model and its scalability is essential. This involves analyzing which parts of your business can be expanded quickly and efficiently, and which parts may require more time and investment to scale. It's crucial to identify your core competencies and focus on areas that offer the most significant growth potential with the least resistance.

Financial management plays a pivotal role in scaling your business. Securing adequate funding to support expansion activities is vital, whether it's through reinvestment of profits, seeking external investment, or accessing business loans. You'll need to forecast financial needs accurately, considering the costs of expanding your team, increasing production capacity, or entering new markets.

Investing in technology can provide the tools necessary for scaling your operations. Automation and digital transformation can streamline processes, enhance productivity, and allow you to serve more customers without a proportional increase in costs. This might involve adopting new software systems, upgrading existing technology infrastructure, or leveraging data analytics to gain insights into customer behavior and market trends.

Human resources are equally critical when scaling a business. As you grow, attracting and retaining the right talent becomes more challenging yet more crucial. You'll need to develop a strong company culture that can scale with your business, implementing systems for training, development, and employee engagement that ensure your team remains motivated and aligned with your business goals. Marketing and sales strategies need to evolve as your business scales. Expanding your customer base and entering new markets require a deep understanding of your target audience and the competitive landscape. Investing in marketing and sales capabilities, such as enhancing your online presence, optimizing your sales funnel, or adopting new sales technologies, can drive growth and improve customer acquisition and retention rates.

Operational efficiency must be maintained or improved as you scale. This means regularly reviewing and optimizing your operations, supply chain, and product or service delivery processes to ensure they can handle increased demand. Streamlining operations can involve everything from renegotiating supplier contracts to implementing quality control systems that maintain product or service standards.

Strategic partnerships and collaborations can also play a crucial role in scaling your business. By aligning with partners that offer complementary products, services, or market access, you can leverage synergies to accelerate growth and expand your reach more effectively than going it alone. Maintaining a customer-centric approach is essential as you scale. The quality of your customer experience should not diminish as your business grows. Instead, you should continuously seek feedback, innovate your offerings, and ensure that your customer service scales alongside your business.

Scaling your business requires a balanced approach, focusing on financial health, technological investment, talent management, operational efficiency, and market expansion, all while maintaining a strong commitment to customer satisfaction. It's a challenging journey, but with the right strategies and mindset, it can lead to significant growth and long-term success.

Strategies for Growth and Expansion

Strategies for growth and expansion in business necessitate a blend of innovation, strategic planning, and keen market insight. To thrive and scale, businesses must not only excel in their current operations but also constantly seek new opportunities and avenues for growth. This approach requires a comprehensive understanding of one's market, customers, and the broader industry trends, coupled with an ability to adapt and innovate continually.

One core strategy for growth involves diving deep into market research to unearth untapped opportunities. This research should encompass understanding emerging trends, customer behavior, and needs, as well as identifying gaps in the market that your business can fill. Armed with this knowledge, a business can tailor its products or services to better meet customer demands, adjust its marketing strategies to reach new segments, or even pivot its business model to capitalize on new opportunities. Expanding the range of products or services is another powerful strategy for growth. This could mean enhancing existing offerings with new features or benefits, introducing entirely new product lines, or branching out into complementary services that add value for your customers. Such diversification not only broadens the appeal of your business to a wider audience but also mitigates the risk of over-reliance on a single product or market.

Exploring new geographic markets is a natural progression for businesses looking to grow. Whether it's expanding nationally or venturing into international markets, new locations can offer fresh customer bases and revenue streams. However, this strategy demands a thorough understanding of the new market's cultural, legal, and economic landscape and often requires adapting your offerings and strategies to suit local preferences and regulations.

Leveraging technology to optimize operations and enhance the customer experience is essential in today's digital age. This might involve adopting new software to streamline internal processes, utilizing data analytics to gain insights into customer behavior, or embracing e-commerce to reach customers beyond your physical location. Technology not only facilitates operational efficiency but can also open up new channels for customer engagement and sales.

Forming strategic partnerships and alliances can provide a significant boost to growth efforts. By collaborating with other businesses, whether through joint ventures, partnerships, or mergers, companies can leverage each other's strengths, share resources, and access new markets or customer segments more effectively than they might on their own.

Investing in marketing and sales is critical to driving business growth. Developing a strong brand presence, optimizing your online visibility, engaging with customers through social media, and employing targeted advertising can all help attract new customers and retain existing ones. An effective sales and marketing strategy should be data-driven, allowing for continuous optimization based on customer feedback and performance metrics. Improving operational efficiencies is another key area of focus for businesses aiming to scale. This could involve refining supply chain management, automating manual processes, or adopting lean manufacturing principles. By reducing waste and improving productivity, businesses can lower costs and increase profitability, creating a solid foundation for sustainable growth.

Fostering a culture of innovation and continuous improvement is vital. Encouraging creativity and innovation within your team, staying open to new ideas, and being willing to take calculated risks can lead to breakthroughs that propel your business forward. A culture that values agility and adaptability is essential for navigating the challenges of growth and seizing new opportunities as they arise.

Hiring Employees or Outsourcing Tasks When Necessary

In the journey of growing a business, there comes a pivotal moment when the need to expand the team or outsource tasks becomes apparent. This decision is crucial for maintaining efficiency, ensuring quality, and fostering innovation. Whether to hire new employees or outsource depends on various factors including the nature of the work, budget constraints, and long-term strategic goals.

Hiring employees is a significant step that involves bringing talents into the organization to become part of the team. This option is particularly appealing when the tasks at hand require a deep understanding of the company's culture, ongoing involvement in its projects, and a commitment to its long-term vision. Having a dedicated team allows for greater control over the work process, fosters team cohesion, and builds a pool of expertise within the company. It's an investment in the company's human capital, which not only contributes to its current projects but also its future endeavors. However, this approach entails considerations of salary, benefits, training, and the infrastructure needed to support additional staff.

On the other hand, outsourcing involves delegating certain tasks or projects to external entities or individuals. This strategy is beneficial for handling specialized tasks that do not necessitate full-time positions or for managing workload peaks without the long-term commitment of hiring an employee. Outsourcing can provide access to a wide range of expertise and innovative solutions that might not be available in-house. It is cost-effective in terms of reducing overhead expenses and offers flexibility to scale operations up or down based on business needs. However, it requires careful selection of partners and clear communication of expectations to ensure the quality and reliability of the outsourced work.

Choosing between hiring and outsourcing often hinges on evaluating the core competencies required for your business's growth and the strategic importance of the tasks. For core activities that are vital to the business's unique value proposition and competitive advantage, hiring may be the preferred route. It ensures that critical skills and knowledge are retained within the company. For specialized or one-off projects, outsourcing can be more practical, allowing the business to tap into external expertise and technology.

Regardless of the choice, both strategies necessitate clear communication, proper management, and alignment with the business's goals and culture. When hiring, it's important to invest in a thorough recruitment process, ensure proper onboarding, and foster ongoing development to build a strong and engaged team. When outsourcing, defining project scopes, timelines, deliverables, and quality standards upfront is key to successful collaboration. Regular reviews and feedback can help maintain alignment and adjust strategies as needed.

Balancing the mix of in-house talent and outsourced partnerships can provide businesses with the flexibility, efficiency, and innovation needed to navigate their growth phases. This balanced approach allows businesses to leverage the strengths of both strategies, optimizing their operations and focusing on their core competencies while accessing external expertise and resources as needed.

Leveraging Technology for Scalability

Leveraging technology for scalability is a strategic approach that enables businesses to expand their operations, reach, and efficiency without a proportional increase in costs. This approach involves adopting and integrating technological solutions that streamline processes, enhance productivity, and improve service delivery. The goal is to create a business infrastructure that can support growth and adapt to changing market demands with agility and minimal friction.

One of the foundational steps in leveraging technology for scalability is the adoption of cloud computing. Cloud services provide businesses with scalable IT resources without the need for significant upfront investment in physical hardware. This flexibility allows businesses to adjust their IT capabilities in line with their current needs, ensuring they can handle growth spurts and increased demand without downtime or performance issues.

Automation plays a crucial role in scalability, particularly in repetitive and time-consuming tasks such as data entry, customer support through chatbots, and inventory management. Automation not only reduces the likelihood of human error but also frees up employee time to focus on more strategic tasks that require human insight. This shift not only improves operational efficiency but also enhances employee satisfaction by elevating the nature of their work.

Data analytics and artificial intelligence (AI) offer powerful tools for businesses aiming to scale. By harnessing data analytics, companies can gain insights into customer behavior, market trends, and operational efficiency. These insights can inform strategic decisions, from product development to marketing strategies, ensuring that businesses remain competitive and responsive to market needs. AI can further enhance scalability by providing personalized customer experiences, optimizing logistics, and predicting market trends, enabling businesses to anticipate and adapt to changes more swiftly.

E-commerce platforms are another technological lever for scalability, especially for retail businesses. These platforms can handle a high volume of transactions and customer interactions, ensuring that businesses can scale their sales operations without compromising customer experience. Moreover, e-commerce technology enables businesses to reach a global market, breaking down geographical barriers to growth.

Customer Relationship Management (CRM) systems are essential for managing interactions with current and potential customers in a scalable way. These systems streamline customer data management, sales tracking, and communication, ensuring that as the business grows, it maintains or improves its level of customer service. A scalable CRM solution supports a growing customer base, ensuring that businesses can manage increased volumes of customer interactions efficiently.

Collaboration tools and project management software facilitate scalable operations by enhancing communication and coordination among teams, regardless of their size or geographical location. These tools ensure that as teams grow, they can continue to collaborate effectively, maintaining productivity and alignment on projects and goals.

In implementing technology for scalability, it's crucial for businesses to adopt a strategic approach that aligns with their specific needs and growth objectives. This involves not only selecting the right technologies but also ensuring they are integrated seamlessly into existing processes and that staff are trained effectively to use them. Furthermore, businesses must stay abreast of emerging technologies and continuously evaluate their tech stack to ensure it supports ongoing growth and efficiency.

Managing Challenges and Risks

Managing challenges and risks is an integral part of running a business, involving the identification, assessment, and mitigation of potential threats to the organization's objectives. This process is crucial for ensuring long-term sustainability and success, as unaddressed risks can lead to financial losses, reputational damage, and even the failure of the business. Effective risk management requires a proactive approach, combining strategic planning, thorough analysis, and adaptive measures.

The first step in managing challenges and risks is to systematically identify potential threats. These can vary widely depending on the nature of the business, industry, market conditions, and other external factors. Common risks include financial uncertainties, legal liabilities, technological changes, competition, market demand shifts, and operational inefficiencies. Identifying risks involves not just looking at current challenges but also anticipating future ones, requiring a deep understanding of the business environment and the ability to think critically about what could go wrong.

Once risks have been identified, the next step is to assess their potential impact and the likelihood of their occurrence. This assessment helps prioritize risks based on their severity and the business's ability to withstand them. Some risks may have a high potential impact but a low likelihood of occurring, while others might be more probable but less damaging. Assessing risks in this way allows businesses to allocate resources more effectively, focusing on preventing or preparing for the most critical threats. Mitigation strategies are then developed and implemented to manage the prioritized risks. Mitigation can take various forms, including avoiding the risk entirely, reducing the likelihood of its occurrence, minimizing its impact, or transferring the risk (for example, through insurance). The chosen strategy should align with the business's overall objectives and risk tolerance. For instance, a business may decide to avoid entering a high-risk market or invest in technology to improve operational efficiency and reduce the risk of errors.

An essential part of managing challenges and risks is establishing a culture of risk awareness throughout the organization. This involves training employees to recognize and respond to risks, encouraging open communication about potential threats, and fostering an environment where risks can be discussed and addressed without fear of blame. Such a culture ensures that risk management is not confined to the upper echelons of the organization but is integrated into every aspect of the business's operations.

Continuous monitoring and review of the risk management process are vital for its effectiveness. The business environment is constantly changing, with new risks emerging and existing ones evolving. Regularly reviewing and updating risk assessments, mitigation strategies, and response plans ensure that the business remains prepared for challenges as they arise. This iterative process allows businesses to adapt to changes in the market, regulatory landscape, or their operational context, maintaining resilience in the face of adversity.

In addition to internal measures, businesses can also manage risks by diversifying their product offerings, markets, and revenue streams. Diversification reduces reliance on a single source of income or market, spreading risk across different areas. This strategy can buffer the business against sector-specific downturns and provide alternative growth avenues during challenging times.

Finally, effective risk management often involves seeking external advice and expertise. This can include consulting with legal experts, financial advisors, and industry specialists who can provide insights into specific risks and how to mitigate them. Collaborating with these experts can enhance the business's understanding of potential challenges and bolster its strategies for managing them.

Managing challenges and risks is a dynamic and ongoing process that is crucial for the stability and growth of any business. By systematically identifying, assessing, and mitigating risks, fostering a culture of risk awareness, continuously monitoring the risk landscape, diversifying operations, and seeking external expertise, businesses can navigate uncertainties more effectively and pave the way for sustainable success.

Common Challenges Faced By In-Home Bookkeeping Services

In-home bookkeeping services, while offering flexibility and lower operational costs, confront a unique set of challenges. These challenges range from securing a steady flow of clients and managing time efficiently to ensuring data security and staying up-to-date with regulatory changes. Understanding these hurdles is the first step in developing strategies to overcome them and ensure the success of an in-home bookkeeping business:

1. Client Acquisition and Retention: One of the primary challenges for in-home bookkeeping services is building and maintaining a robust client base. With the proliferation of bookkeeping services, standing out in a crowded market can be difficult. Furthermore,

retaining clients requires consistently delivering high-quality service, meeting deadlines, and providing added value to discourage clients from switching to competitors or adopting do-it-yourself bookkeeping software.

2. Data Security and Privacy: Handling sensitive financial information imposes a significant responsibility on bookkeepers to ensure data security and privacy. In an in-home setting, implementing robust cybersecurity measures and physical security protocols to protect client data can be more challenging and costly. The risk of data breaches or loss due to hardware issues, cyberattacks, or inadequate security practices can lead to significant reputational damage and legal consequences.

3. Time Management and Work-Life Balance: Managing time efficiently is crucial for in-home bookkeepers who must balance client work, business administration, and personal life. Without clear boundaries, the flexibility of working from home can lead to overwork or distractions, impacting productivity and the quality of work. Establishing a structured schedule and maintaining a dedicated workspace within the home can help, but it requires discipline and organization.

4. Keeping Up with Technological Advances: The field of bookkeeping is continuously evolving, with new software and technologies enhancing how bookkeeping services are delivered.

Staying abreast of these changes and mastering new tools can be time-consuming and expensive. However, failing to keep up with technological advances can leave in-home bookkeepers at a competitive disadvantage.

5. Compliance with Laws and Regulations: Bookkeeping involves navigating complex tax laws and financial regulations, which can change frequently. Keeping up-to-date with these changes and ensuring compliance to avoid penalties for both the bookkeeper and their clients is a constant challenge. This requires ongoing education and possibly consultation with legal experts, which can be both time-consuming and costly.

6. Managing Cash Flow: For many in-home bookkeepers, particularly those just starting out or operating as solo practitioners, managing cash flow can be challenging. Irregular income streams, late payments from clients, and the need to set aside funds for taxes, software subscriptions, and professional development can strain financial resources. Effective financial planning and establishing clear payment terms with clients are essential for maintaining a healthy cash flow.

7. Professional Isolation: Working from home, especially as a sole practitioner, can lead to feelings of isolation and disconnection from the professional community. This isolation can impact mental health and reduce opportunities for networking, collaboration, and

professional growth. Actively seeking out professional associations, online communities, and local networking events can help mitigate these feelings and provide valuable support and opportunities for collaboration.

Overcoming these challenges requires strategic planning, adaptability, and a commitment to professional development. By effectively addressing these hurdles, in-home bookkeeping services can thrive, providing valuable financial management solutions to their clients while enjoying the flexibility and autonomy of working from home.

Strategies for Overcoming Obstacles and Staying Resilient

Overcoming obstacles and staying resilient in the face of challenges are crucial skills for individuals and businesses alike. The ability to navigate difficulties, adapt to change, and emerge stronger from adversity is what defines resilience. Implementing strategies to build and maintain resilience can help in managing stress, making informed decisions, and pursuing growth despite uncertainties.

 Here are some effective strategies for overcoming obstacles and bolstering resilience:

Cultivate a Positive Mindset: Resilience begins with the mental fortitude to face challenges head-on. Cultivating a positive mindset helps in viewing obstacles as opportunities for growth and learning rather than insurmountable problems. Embracing optimism, practicing gratitude, and maintaining a sense of humor can lighten the burden of stress and inspire creative problem-solving.

Build a Strong Support Network: No one overcomes challenges in isolation. Having a strong support network of family, friends, mentors, and professional colleagues provides emotional support, practical advice, and different perspectives on problems. Networking and building relationships within your industry can also offer insights into how others have navigated similar challenges.

Embrace Adaptability: The ability to adapt to changing circumstances is a hallmark of resilience. This means being open to new ideas, willing to change course when necessary, and flexible in your approach to problem-solving. Cultivating adaptability involves continuously learning new skills, staying informed about industry trends, and being open to feedback.

Set Realistic Goals and Take Action: Overcoming obstacles often requires breaking down larger challenges into smaller, manageable goals. Setting realistic, achievable goals provides a roadmap for action and a sense of accomplishment as you progress. Taking decisive action towards these goals, even in small steps, builds momentum and confidence.

Practice Self-Care: Resilience is not just about pushing through; it's also about knowing when to step back and recharge. Regular exercise, adequate sleep, healthy eating, and mindfulness practices like meditation can improve physical and mental well-being, enhancing your ability to cope with stress and recover from setbacks.

Learn from Failures: Viewing failures as learning opportunities rather than defeats is critical for resilience. Analyzing what went wrong, understanding the factors that contributed to the outcome, and applying these lessons in the future can transform setbacks into valuable experiences that contribute to growth and improvement.

Maintain Financial Flexibility: For businesses, financial resilience is key to overcoming economic challenges. This means maintaining a healthy cash flow, having access to emergency funds or credit, and being prudent with expenditures. Diversifying income streams and regularly reviewing financial strategies can also provide stability in uncertain times.

Seek Professional Help When Needed: Sometimes, overcoming obstacles may require expertise beyond your current capabilities. Seeking professional help, whether consulting with industry experts, hiring skilled professionals, or accessing mental health resources, can provide the support and guidance needed to navigate complex challenges.

Focus on What You Can Control: In any challenging situation, there are factors within your control and those beyond it. Focusing your energy and efforts on what you can control, such as your attitude, actions, and decisions, empowers you to make positive changes and mitigate the impact of external challenges.

Building and maintaining resilience is a continuous process that requires mindfulness, determination, and the willingness to grow. By implementing these strategies, individuals and businesses can develop the resilience needed to face challenges with confidence, adapt to change, and emerge stronger on the other side.

Risk Management and Contingency Planning

Risk management and contingency planning are essential components of strategic planning for businesses and organizations, providing a framework for identifying, assessing, and mitigating risks. This proactive approach ensures that potential issues are managed and controlled before they become significant problems, enabling the organization to maintain stability and achieve its objectives even in the face of adversity.

Risk Management: An Overview

Risk management involves the identification, analysis, and prioritization of risks followed by the application of resources to minimize, control, or eliminate the impact of unforeseen events.

The process is cyclical and includes several key steps:

-Risk Identification: The first step involves recognizing potential risks that could negatively affect the organization. These can be internal or external, ranging from financial uncertainties, legal liabilities, management errors, accidents, and natural disasters to strategic management errors, technological changes, and competition.

- Risk Assessment: Once identified, each risk is evaluated to determine its potential impact and the likelihood of its occurrence. This assessment helps in prioritizing risks based on their severity and guides the allocation of resources to address them effectively.

- Risk Mitigation Strategies: For each significant risk, mitigation strategies are developed. These strategies may involve avoiding the risk, reducing the risk's potential impact, transferring the risk (e.g., through insurance), or accepting the risk if it's unavoidable and preparing for its consequences.

- Implementation and Monitoring: The chosen risk mitigation strategies are implemented, and their effectiveness is continuously monitored and reviewed. This step ensures that the risk management plan remains relevant and effective over time, allowing for adjustments as the business environment and organizational priorities evolve.

Contingency Planning: An Overview

Contingency planning goes hand-in-hand with risk management, focusing on preparing the organization to respond effectively to significant adverse events or emergencies. Contingency plans outline specific actions to be taken in response to various scenarios, ensuring that the organization can continue operations or recover as quickly and smoothly as possible.

- Scenario Analysis: This involves identifying potential emergencies or adverse events and the conditions under which they would occur. Scenarios could range from natural disasters and cyber-attacks to key staff departures and supply chain disruptions.

- Developing Response Plans: For each identified scenario, a detailed plan is developed, outlining the steps to be taken before, during, and after the event. This includes identifying key personnel responsible for executing the plan, communication strategies, and resources required.

- Testing and Revising Plans: Contingency plans are tested through drills or simulations to ensure their effectiveness and to familiarize staff with their roles in an emergency. Plans are then revised based on feedback and lessons learned during these exercises.

- Regular Review and Updating: Like risk management plans, contingency plans should be regularly reviewed and updated to reflect changes in the organization's structure, operations, and external environment. This ensures that they remain relevant and effective over time.

Integrating Risk Management and Contingency Planning

Integrating risk management and contingency planning into the organizational culture and strategic planning processes is crucial. This integration ensures that all levels of the organization are aware of potential risks and are prepared to respond effectively. Effective communication, ongoing training, and engagement of stakeholders are key components of a successful integration, fostering a proactive and resilient organizational mindset.

Together, risk management and contingency planning equip organizations to navigate uncertainties and challenges more effectively, minimizing potential disruptions and losses while maximizing stability and growth opportunities. This strategic approach enhances an organization's resilience, adaptability, and overall competitiveness.

Continuous Learning and Professional Development

Continuous learning and professional development are pivotal for individuals and organizations aiming to maintain a competitive edge and adapt to the rapidly changing business landscape. This commitment to ongoing education and skill enhancement is not just about personal growth; it's a strategic imperative in today's fast-paced, technology-driven world. By fostering a culture of learning, businesses can innovate, improve efficiency, and enhance their adaptability to new challenges and opportunities.

For Individuals

Continuous learning for individuals involves actively seeking new knowledge, skills, and experiences to enhance their professional capabilities and personal development. This can take various forms, including formal education, workshops, online courses, conferences, self-study, and experiential learning.

The benefits are multifaceted:

- Skill Enhancement: Keeping skills up-to-date with industry trends and technological advancements ensures individuals remain relevant and valuable in their roles.

- Career Advancement: Acquiring new skills and knowledge can open up opportunities for career progression, whether it's taking on more complex projects, moving into leadership positions, or transitioning to new roles or industries.

- Increased Adaptability: Continuous learning equips individuals with a broader skill set and a more versatile approach to problem-solving, making it easier to adapt to changes and overcome challenges.

- Personal Fulfillment: Learning new things can be inherently rewarding, fostering a sense of achievement, confidence, and personal growth.

For Organizations

For organizations, investing in continuous learning and professional development for employees is key to driving innovation, improving productivity, and retaining talent.

Strategies include:

Training Programs: Offering in-house training sessions, workshops, or access to online learning platforms enables employees to develop new skills and knowledge relevant to their roles.

Mentorship and Coaching: Establishing mentorship or coaching programs can facilitate knowledge sharing and personal development, helping employees navigate career paths and work towards their professional goals.

Learning Resources: Providing resources such as books, subscriptions to industry publications, or funding for external courses and certifications encourages self-directed learning and development.

Creating a Learning Culture: Promoting an organizational culture that values curiosity, experimentation, and knowledge sharing fosters a proactive approach to learning and development.

Recognizing and rewarding learning achievements can further reinforce this culture.

Integrating Continuous Learning into Daily Routines

Integrating learning into daily routines ensures that professional development becomes a consistent part of individuals' and organizations' practices rather than an occasional activity. This can involve setting aside dedicated time for learning, encouraging collaborative learning projects, or incorporating learning objectives into performance evaluations.

Challenges and Solutions

While the importance of continuous learning is widely recognized, individuals and organizations may face challenges in implementing effective learning strategies. Time constraints, budget limitations, and uncertainty about which skills to develop can hinder learning efforts. Solutions may include prioritizing learning initiatives based on strategic goals, leveraging free or low-cost online resources, and creating personalized learning plans that align with individual career aspirations and organizational needs.

Continuous learning and professional development are essential for navigating the complexities of the modern workplace, driving innovation, and achieving long-term success. By committing to a lifelong learning journey, individuals and organizations can remain agile, forward-thinking, and equipped to face the future with confidence.

Importance of Staying Updated With Industry Trends and Regulations

Staying updated with industry trends and regulations is critical for businesses and professionals striving to maintain competitiveness, ensure compliance, and drive innovation. In a rapidly evolving marketplace, being well-informed about the latest developments within your industry can provide a strategic advantage, helping to anticipate changes, adapt business strategies accordingly, and seize new opportunities.

Here's a deeper look into why staying updated is so crucial:

Enhancing Competitiveness: Understanding current trends allows businesses to align their products, services, and marketing strategies with consumer demands and preferences. This knowledge can differentiate a business from its competitors, attract more customers, and retain existing ones by offering relevant and innovative solutions.

Ensuring Compliance: Many industries are subject to strict regulatory environments that can change frequently. Staying informed about the latest regulations and legal requirements is essential to avoid costly fines, legal issues, and reputational damage. It also ensures that businesses operate ethically and responsibly, fostering trust with customers, partners, and regulators.

Driving Innovation: By keeping abreast of new technologies, methodologies, and practices within your industry, you can identify opportunities for innovation and improvement. This could involve adopting new technologies to streamline operations, entering emerging markets, or developing new products and services that meet untapped customer needs.

Risk Management: Being aware of industry trends and regulatory changes helps businesses anticipate and manage potential risks more effectively. This includes risks related to market shifts, technological advancements, and new regulatory requirements, enabling businesses to develop proactive strategies to mitigate these risks.

Professional Development: For individuals, staying informed about industry trends and regulations is key to personal and professional growth. It enhances job performance, supports career advancement, and increases employability by ensuring skills and knowledge remain relevant and up-to-date.

Strategic Planning: Informed decision-making is at the heart of successful strategic planning. Understanding the direction in which your industry is headed, along with the regulatory landscape, enables businesses to make strategic investments, allocate resources wisely, and plan for the future with greater clarity and confidence.

Building Authority and Thought Leadership: Professionals and businesses that are knowledgeable about the latest trends and regulations can establish themselves as thought leaders and authoritative voices within their industry. This can enhance brand reputation, facilitate networking opportunities, and attract business opportunities.

How to Stay Updated

1. Subscriptions and Publications: Subscribe to industry journals, magazines, and newsletters that provide insights and updates on trends and regulations.

2. Professional Associations: Join industry associations or organizations for networking opportunities and access to resources, conferences, and workshops.

3. Conferences and Seminars: Attend relevant industry conferences, seminars, and webinars to learn from experts and engage with peers.

4. Online Courses and Training: Enroll in online courses and training programs to enhance your skills and knowledge in specific areas relevant to your industry.

5. Networking: Engage with peers, mentors, and industry leaders through social media, professional networking sites, and industry events to exchange insights and experiences.

6. Regulatory Bodies: Follow regulatory bodies and government agencies relevant to your industry for updates on laws and regulations.

Staying updated with industry trends and regulations is indispensable for navigating the complexities of today's business environment. It empowers businesses and professionals to make informed decisions, remain competitive, and drive meaningful innovation.

Participating In Professional Development Activities

Participating in professional development activities is a vital strategy for individuals aiming to enhance their skills, broaden their knowledge base, and advance their careers. These activities span a wide range of opportunities, including workshops, seminars, conferences, certification programs, and online courses, each designed to meet diverse learning needs and professional goals. Engaging in professional development not only benefits individuals by increasing their competency and competitiveness but also offers substantial advantages to organizations by elevating the overall skill level of their workforce.

For Individuals

1. Skill Enhancement: Continuous learning through professional development activities ensures that individuals keep pace with the latest industry standards, technologies, and best practices. This is particularly crucial in fast-evolving fields where new tools and methodologies can significantly impact job performance and opportunities for advancement.

2. Career Growth: Actively participating in professional development can open doors to career progression, making individuals eligible for promotions or qualifying them for new roles. Employers often look for candidates who demonstrate a commitment to continuous learning as it shows initiative, adaptability, and a drive to excel.

3. Networking Opportunities: Many professional development activities provide platforms for networking with peers, industry leaders, and potential mentors. These connections can be invaluable for sharing knowledge, discovering job opportunities, and building professional relationships that may lead to collaborations or new career paths.

4. Certification and Licensing: Certain professions require ongoing education to maintain licensure or certifications. Participating in accredited professional development programs can fulfill these requirements, ensuring individuals remain qualified to practice in their respective fields.

5. Personal Fulfillment: Learning new skills or deepening existing knowledge can be personally rewarding, boosting confidence and reigniting passion for one's work. This intrinsic motivation often translates into improved job satisfaction and performance.

For Organizations

1. Enhanced Competitiveness: By encouraging and facilitating professional development, organizations can nurture a highly skilled workforce capable of driving innovation, improving efficiency, and maintaining a competitive edge in the marketplace.

2. Employee Retention: Investing in employees' professional growth can increase their loyalty and job satisfaction, reducing turnover rates. Employees are more likely to stay with an organization that values their development and provides opportunities for advancement.

3. Adaptability: A culture of continuous learning equips organizations to adapt more readily to industry changes and challenges. A well-informed and agile workforce can pivot more easily in response to new trends, technologies, and market demands.

4. Quality Improvement: Professional development activities often lead to improvements in work quality as employees apply new knowledge and techniques to their roles. This can result in higher productivity, better customer service, and enhanced overall performance.

Implementing Professional Development

To fully benefit from professional development activities, both individuals and organizations should adopt a strategic approach. This includes setting clear learning goals, selecting relevant opportunities aligned with career objectives or business strategies, and applying new skills and knowledge in practical settings. Additionally, fostering a supportive culture that values education and development can enhance engagement and participation in these activities.

Participating in professional development activities is a crucial element of career and organizational growth. It fosters a culture of continuous improvement, ensuring that individuals and teams remain relevant, responsive, and capable of contributing to their fullest potential.

Networking With Other Bookkeeping Professionals and Organizations

Networking with other bookkeeping professionals and organizations is a strategic approach that can significantly enhance a bookkeeper's career and the operational success of their bookkeeping practice. This involves building relationships with individuals and organizations within the bookkeeping and broader financial industry to exchange knowledge, share resources, and collaborate on opportunities. The benefits of networking in this field are extensive and can lead to professional growth, business development, and continuous learning.

Knowledge Sharing and Learning

Networking allows bookkeepers to share insights, experiences, and best practices with peers. This exchange can be invaluable for staying informed about the latest industry trends, software updates, and regulatory changes. Through discussions, workshops, and seminars that often accompany networking events, professionals can learn from the successes and challenges of others, gaining new perspectives and solutions that can be applied to their own practice.

Access to Resources and Tools

Connections made through networking can provide access to a wide array of resources and tools that may not be readily available otherwise. This includes specialized software, templates, and methodologies that have been tested and recommended by peers. Additionally, professional associations often provide members with exclusive resources, such as research publications, industry reports, and educational materials, which can further enhance a bookkeeper's practice.

Referral Opportunities

One of the most direct benefits of networking is the potential for referral business. Building a strong network of fellow professionals and industry contacts can lead to referrals when others encounter clients that require specialized bookkeeping services or when they are unable to take on additional work themselves. These referrals are particularly valuable as they come with the endorsement of the referrer, providing a level of trust and credibility from the outset.

Collaboration and Support

Networking can lead to opportunities for collaboration on larger projects or the formation of partnerships that expand service offerings. For bookkeepers running their own practice, this can mean the ability to take on more substantial clients or projects by teaming up with others who have complementary skills or resources. Additionally, having a network of peers provides a support system for problem-solving, advice, and encouragement, which can be especially beneficial during challenging times.

Professional Development and Career Advancement

Engaging with professional organizations, attending conferences, and participating in continuing education sessions not only contribute to a bookkeeper's professional development but also signal a commitment to excellence and a proactive approach to career advancement. Networking in these environments can lead to mentorship opportunities, advanced training, and even job offers or career changes as professionals become aware of your skills and dedication to the field.

How to Network Effectively

Effective networking requires a strategic approach:

Join Professional Associations: Become active in bookkeeping and accounting associations such as the National Association of Certified Public Bookkeepers (NACPB) or the American Institute of Professional Bookkeepers (AIPB). Attend their events, participate in forums, and volunteer for committees.

Attend Industry Conferences: Conferences and seminars are excellent places to meet peers, learn about industry trends, and engage with thought leaders.

Leverage Social Media: Platforms like LinkedIn provide opportunities to connect with other bookkeeping professionals, join industry-specific groups, and share knowledge.

Offer Help Generously: Networking is a two-way street. Offer your expertise and support to others without immediately expecting something in return. This builds goodwill and establishes you as a valuable member of the community.

Conclusion

The journey through various facets of professional growth, from leveraging technology for scalability, managing challenges and risks, to the importance of continuous learning, professional development activities, and networking, underscores a comprehensive roadmap for success in today's dynamic business environment. Each element, while distinct in its focus, interconnects to form a holistic strategy for individuals and organizations aiming to not only survive but thrive amidst the complexities of modern industries.

Technology stands as a pivotal enabler of scalability, offering tools and platforms that can transform operational efficiency, customer engagement, and competitive positioning. Embracing digital advancements is no longer optional but a critical determinant of growth and sustainability.

Risk management and contingency planning emerge as essential practices, safeguarding businesses against potential pitfalls and ensuring they can navigate uncertainties with confidence. These strategies underscore the importance of foresight, preparation, and adaptability in securing a firm's future.

Continuous learning and professional development represent the lifeblood of personal and organizational advancement. In an era marked by rapid technological changes and shifting market demands, the commitment to ongoing education and skill enhancement is what enables professionals and businesses to remain relevant, innovative, and ahead of the curve.

Networking, particularly for specialized professionals such as bookkeepers, opens a realm of opportunities for knowledge exchange, collaboration, and business growth. It highlights the power of community and mutual support in fostering professional success and resilience.

Together, these components weave a narrative that champions proactive growth strategies, resilience in the face of challenges, and the relentless pursuit of excellence. Whether for individuals charting their career paths or businesses striving for market leadership, the integration of these strategies paves the way for achieving lasting success and making a meaningful impact in their respective domains.

www.ingramcontent.com/pod-product-compliance
Lightning Source LLC
Chambersburg PA
CBHW071919210526
45479CB00002B/476